Never Sleep Three in a Bed

Never Sleep Three in a Bed

Max Braithwaite

McClelland and Stewart Limited

Also by Max Braithwaite:

The Muffled Man
The Valley of the Vanishing Birds
Voices of the Wild
Land of Water and People
Why Shoot the Teacher?
The Night We Stole The Mountie's Car

Revised edition 1975

The Canadian Publishers
McClelland and Stewart Limited
25 Hollinger Road, Toronto

ISBN: 0-7710-1606-9

PRINTED AND BOUND IN CANADA

Contents

To Mother,

whose indomitable spirit, strength, love and humour pulled us through the bad time.

To Dad,

who made the whole family possible.

To my four brothers and three sisters,

who have been so much a part of my life.

1 *Nokomis—"Best in the West"*

Whenever I hear talk of the population explosion, the desperate need for birth-control or the pill, I am troubled. I look away and cough and scratch my rump, and try to switch the conversation to Vietnam or something equally uncontroversial. For I happen to be the sixth in a family of eight children, and had my parents been wiser, or more cautious, or better informed on family planning, I should never have been born at all. And I should have hated that.

My mother has since admitted to me that she looked forward to my coming with something less than jubilation. She'd had five already within a period of seven years, and had been hoping for a few years off. But what was the poor woman to do? She loved her husband, and a body can't be careful all the time. Nevertheless, once I arrived she loved me and cared for me, and I'm grateful for it.

Our family wasn't a big one as families went during the first quarter of the century, just a comfortable size. Ten at the table for each meal is a good round number, and five boys and three girls is a fair and equitable balance of the sexes. I've heard my sister Doris dispute this when she was in a snit over something "those boys" had done or said, but then she might be considered prejudiced.

I was born in the middle of the night in the dead of

winter, in the midst of a real cold snap. Doc Brown, who had to drag himself out of bed, pull on his fur cap and buffalo-hide coat and mitts, and trudge the three blocks to our house through the snapping cold, is reported to have grumbled, "Don't see why those damned Braithwaite kids can't be born in the summer. All but one's been a winter baby!"

When he got upstairs to the cold front bedroom, where my mother lay gasping in the big wooden bed, and pulled me from the warmth of her body I naturally began to howl. I continued to howl, too, almost constantly they say, so as almost to drive my mother mad. The truth was, of course, that I was hungry, and there wasn't enough nourishment in my tired mother's breasts to satisfy me. After all, the care of five small children, along with the chores of fetching water, carrying coal, stoking fires, feeding chickens, washing by hand, baking bread and preserving crab-apples had taken something out of her. Bottle-feeding being on the long list of Methodist sins I continued to hunger and howl.

That howling, as a matter of fact, almost brought me to a premature end. When Mother was well enough to travel, Father, who was a rising young lawyer in the fastest-growing town in the fastest-growing province in the West, decided to take her, and what kids couldn't be left behind, on the C.P.R. to the West Coast. The other kids weren't that much trouble, but I was a holy terror. The mountain air made me hungrier, and I bawled louder. Day and night I bawled, without let-up, single-lungedly ruining the trip for a Pullman car full of tourists. My poor mother was so distracted that as she stood by the railing of the ferry-boat carrying us across Georgia Strait my sister Doris heard her mutter, "Hush, you little demon, or I've a good mind to drop you overboard." Doris, a sober seven-year-old, who took her duties as eldest girl seriously, was in such a panic for the rest of the trip that she refused to leave Mother's side, lest she really did carry out this horrible threat. Come to think of it, I probably owe my life to Doris.

The effect of my early hunger left a life-long mark upon me. For no sooner was I able to reach for food, or find it, or steal it, than I began cramming it into my mouth as though there would never be any more. As a natural consequence I became fat, and portliness has been the key to my personality development ever since.

Each of us in this life has his own division of people. The black power advocate sees all humans as black or white. The communist sees them as rich or poor. The feminist sees the world as made up of mean men and good women; the WASP sees them as pure and impure; the French Canadian as exploiter and exploitee, and so on.

Well, the fat man sees the world as divided into two classes – lean and stout. The lean resent the stout, scoff at them, humiliate them and, I'm sure if they were able, would pass discriminatory laws against them. They also assume that each pudgy person yearns to be slim, which is of course absolute nonsense. All the fat person wants is to be accepted as a *person*, to be treated as an individual, to be greeted by old acquaintances with a simple, "Hello there, fellow, how's tricks?" instead of, "Putting on a little lard there around the middle aren't you, old boy?"

Thus, early in life, I learned to regard all skinny persons as natural enemies, out to get me. There is nothing paranoid in this, you understand. Nevertheless, it does seem odd that every teacher, doctor, scoutmaster, policeman, producer, director, editor or publisher with whom I've had to deal in my entire life has had a lean and hungry look, and has been definitely dangerous.

Early on, my brother Hub tagged me with the nickname "Fat", and after that I was forced to lick every new kid that called me by that opprobrious label. Thus, what might well have been an individual with a gentle, loving, out-going nature was transformed into a vicious, mean, thin-skinned wretch, ever quick to take offence, and to snap suspiciously even at the hand extended in friendship.

And it all began at my mother's breast.

The house in which I was born was large and square, and stood on the edge of the town of Nokomis, Saskatchewan. It was made of cement blocks, but for some reason has always been referred to by the family as the "old stone house". It was built as a hospital, when the town was first established in 1905, by two civic-minded ladies from Chicago. According to a historical booklet, the corner-stone was laid with a short religious service, and the band of the Royal Templars provided "open air entertainment." While the Grand Trunk Railway was being built the hospital did a good business in broken bones, crushed feet, squeezed-off hands and frost-bite, but after the railway was finished trade fell off, the good ladies returned to Chicago, and Dad bought the house for his expanding family. "The way kids keep getting sick," he's reported to have said, "a hospital will be just the thing."

The house was surrounded by a yard about an acre in size. Part of it was lawn, surrounded by box-elder trees which we called Manitoba maples, and part of it garden with currant bushes, with whose lush fruit I stuffed myself every season. The rest was taken up with barn, chicken-coop, pig-pen and, of course, a two-holer off to the side, painted a discreet brown and partly hidden by trees. Behind the barn, a wheat field stretched to the horizon, without a hill or tree or stone to break its flatness.

That yard was ever full of life. Long-legged grasshoppers leaped in the grass, chickweed and pigweed that covered the area between house and barn. Big busy chickens roamed at will, chasing the grasshoppers and pecking viciously at unwary toads. One of my earliest recollections is of the big bronze rooster, lifting his head high, cocking his beady eye, and then tearing across the barnyard to jump a hen amidst flying feathers and fearful squawking. How he knew which one was ready I never figured, but I never tired of watching his torrid dash to fulfilment. No nonsense there. He showed those hens which was the dominant sex, all right.

Cats were forever having kittens in the soft hay of the barn. Bitches had pups, sows had litters, cows had calves, mares had colts. No need to show us self-conscious little films of male frogs clutching females, and releasing their sperm on the emerging eggs. Raw sex was all about us, natural and constant.

Inside the barn was the domain of Kate and Harry, two lean, shaggy work-horses that Father had acquired through some kind of deal. He kept them, I suppose, because of the always imminent prospect that he would move to a farm. Farms were everything in Saskatchewan then. Like oil became in Alberta later. If you didn't have a farm, and weren't getting in on those big wheat prices, you were a sloven indeed. Father did actually try farming a little later, with results so disastrous as to still make us squirm. After paying top prices for the ploughing, cultivating and seeding, he watched his wheat grow to a bumper crop that was completely wiped out by frost before he ever put a binder into it.

There was another horse in that barn, too, a driver named Old Tom, whom my older brothers described as a "kidney stallion". I never knew exactly what that meant, but it seems Old Tom was neither completely stud nor gelding, and could get very excited over a mare in the proper mood.

Old Tom distinguished himself in my memory by walking one hot day into the middle of the slough behind the barn, and lying down in it. A stupid thing to do, but I suppose that's the price one pays for being half-and-half. Anyway, when he'd cooled off sufficiently and tried to get up, he couldn't. I stood with a group of my elders, listening to their joking remarks about his helpless wallowings, and I was scared. Tom was our friend, just as Old Girlie, the cat, was our friend, and Patsy, the dog, and for that matter the other members of our family. And here he was in danger of death. Death, that horror that haunts all little boys. He might actually die. Surely people should be more distressed by the prospect. There should be more urgency, more panic. They shouldn't just stand there, hands in pockets, joking.

I'll never forget what happened next, either. Somebody threw a rope over Old Tom's head and hitched Kate and Harry to the other end of it. The team pulled, and Tom's neck began to stretch. I can see it now–stretching and stretching–until I was sure his head would come from his body. Then with a mighty effort he scrambled from the ooze to his feet, walked out of the slough under his own power, and commenced nibbling the grass at the edge.

Thus a boy learns the facts of life. I remember the day two strange, dark men came to visit Kate's colt. They told me to beat it, and closed the barn door tight. I peeked through a knot-hole into the dusty dankness, and made out one man sitting on the colt's head while the other did terrible things to its other end. Then they went to the pig-pen and performed the same operation on the spunky young boars. They weren't quiet as the colt had been, and their horrible, heart-broken squeals rang in my head for days.

In the barn, also, lived a red cow with a crumpled horn. Her name was Old Rosie. She was remarkable in that she never freshened. It's a known fact that a cow should have a calf once a year, in order to keep her mammary glands functioning for the benefit of humans. Not so Old Rosie. She never had a calf, either while we lived in Nokomis or after we moved to Prince Albert, but still she continued to give a pailful of milk each day. Farmers would come for miles to see her. They'd stand beside the stall, scratching their rumps and shaking their heads. "It just ain't possible," they'd say.

Of all my friends in Nokomis, Old Rosie was not among my favourites. Oh, I liked to stand and watch Morley milk her, meanwhile shooting long streams of warm milk into the pink mouths of lurking kittens. I liked to listen to him swear at her when she switched her tail in his face until he finally got mad enough to tie it to her hind leg. But she butted me in the forehead once, and would make little runs at me when Hub was taking her out to be tethered behind the barn. Besides, despite my gluttonous appetite for other foods, I was never able to drink milk.

There were three hundred and seventy-four people living in Nokomis when I arrived there, and none had been in the community more than six years. There hadn't *been* any community six years earlier, just the flat prairie and the grass and the gophers. Thus, everything in the village was brand-new. The wooden sidewalks, the little trim brick-red station, the four grain elevators along the tracks, the houses, the stores, the trees – all new.

The people were new, too. A community without an old-timer. All the adults were there from choice, having sought out this little part of the world for reasons best known to themselves. Some, to get away from bad situations at home; others, lured by garish posters that promised free homesteads in a land "where none need call another master and where the wealth of the soil is for the hardy to take".

But mostly they came because they were restless. Tired of the same old faces and rules, wanting something different. The same reasons that have always goaded men to travel and explore and experiment. They came to Saskatchewan because it was there – and new – and unknown.

From the United States they came, from Ontario, the

British Isles, Germany, Central Europe. It was a duke's mixture of races, cultures and languages. My earliest recollections are of people speaking strange tongues. They had no time for racial or religious bigotry–that would come later. My father, for instance, who'd been a staunch member of the Orange Lodge in Ontario, as had been his father and grandfathers before him, put his uniform with the great orange sash away in a box and left it there. We kids would get it out and play with it, wondering idly what it was all about.

The people of Nokomis were enthusiastic about their new community, too, and had great faith in its future. For wasn't it situated in the middle of the best black-soil region in the West? And wasn't it located exactly three hundred and eighty-five miles west of Winnipeg, the "Gateway to the West"? Not three hundred and seventy-five miles like Tate, or three hundred and ninety-five like Venn, those two neighbours who foolishly thought *they* would become the great metropolises of the West. And wasn't this the perfect place for a town–flat and smooth, without even a hill to mar its beauty? Plenty of underground water there, too. The real estate people guaranteed it. You'd have to dig deep, maybe, and it might taste like epsom salts when you got it, but it was there all right.

Dad and Mother had come west like the others, seeking and escaping. Mother's father, James Copeland, was a young red-bearded Irishman, from County Armagh, with itchy feet. He emigrated to Ontario, and in the town of Winchester met and married a likely Irish girl by the name of Arabell Timmins. Further west they went to Dundalk, in Grey County, and established a farm. But the western winds were blowing word of wider plains and richer soil than the swamp and gravel around Dundalk. So James packed his family on one of the first trains going west, and stayed with her as far as the rails went. This was the Summerberry area, in the District of Assiniboia (now southern Saskatchewan). They raised eleven children, did James and Arabell Copeland, never lost a one, and they all grew up to have numerous children of their own.

Mary, my mother, was just an infant when the family moved west, and remembered little of the trip. She grew up working hard on the farm, a pert ragamuffin of a girl, with a lively wit and a serene Methodist conviction that God would watch over her and hers, if she were good. God had led her to the prairies, she believed, to meet Warner and, after she met him, the aggravating winds, the mean winters, the parched summers and the cruel times didn't matter at all.

I realize that in this mother-debunking age I'll be put down as a square if I say anything good about mine. So I'll just let the facts speak for themselves. She raised eight kids and never lost one of them. None of us was ever in jail, in a divorce court, or on a psychiatrist's couch. She knew no child-psychology, had never heard of Gessel *et al*, and never used the word "relate" or "aggression" or "inhibition" in her life. When a kid was good, she rewarded him with love and smiles; when a kid was bad or saucy, she whacked him. Simple justice. If she happened to whack the wrong kid–well, she'd make up for it next time.

She made us do plenty of things we didn't want to do, filled us with guilt feelings about not attending Sunday School, swearing or drinking, and being sinful with girls. She even scared the devil out of us with stories of goblins that came after little boys who didn't say their prayers. She had a strong conviction that she was right, because wasn't God on her side, and wasn't He always right? Most important of all, she had the indomitable spirit of motherhood. She just wouldn't give up. Not ever. When times got tough, she got tougher. Yes, she had to humiliate herself sometimes, lying to bill collectors, and working like a dog calsomining rooms after each roomer left, but she kept us at a good address, and never let us forget what was "decent".

And she never blamed her Warner for any of the bad times. She knew he was the best and kindest man alive, and that was that.

Warner, his full name was George Albert Warner, went West, I'm sure, to get free of a stern Middlesex County Victorian family and two domineering older sisters. Born on a farm, he was still no farmer, just as his father, George, son of Thomas, who had emigrated from Armagh years earlier, was no farmer. Warner went to the old Model School on Gould Street in Toronto, and taught in a small school in Ontario for a spell. Then a friend told him that teachers were in great demand in the new territories, and a man could make a fortune buying and selling farms. So, he left his family, some of whom he never saw again, and went West.

He was a tall, lean young man, with a dashing black moustache and a deep voice. To bring a little culture to the farmers in the school district near Summerberry where he taught, he gave poetry readings in the evenings. Byron, mostly, and Keats–the fiery romantics. Mary heard him and, just as in the story books, fell head over heels. And he fell for her, too, and from that time on wanted no other woman. So they were married in Grenfell a week before Christmas, in 1901. He was within a month of being thirty-four years old, and she was twenty-five. They vowed to love each other through sickness and health and for better or for worse and–by gawd!–that's what they did.

At first it was all adventure. Warner didn't want to be a teacher, not really, so he studied law at night and on the weekends until he was admitted to the bar, and became one of the province's first lawyers. Then he looked around for some town where the action was. Naturally, he picked on Nokomis– wasn't it the fastest growing community in the West? After all, from nothing to a population of three hundred plus within three years is a truly phenomenal rate of growth.

Down on the main street, between McEwen's store and the bank, Warner built a one-storey frame office with a big desk and a notary's seal that made funny raised marks on paper. There was plenty of legal work in the booming community. Somebody was always suing somebody else over property lines, water rights, and so on, and there were a lot of deeds to register. Being a friendly, capable man with no racial bigotry, Dad fitted well into the polyglot population and prospered. He once told me that he cleared ten dollars a day, and that was plenty to raise a family on.

My father licked me only once in those Nokomis days and according to his lights I sure deserved it.

It was the stick-horses that got me into trouble. Stick-horses – now there was a game. It required absolutely nothing bought at the store, or given to you at Christmas time, just some willow-gads cut from around the slough. The slim ones became driving-horses, the heavy ones powerful work-horses – Clydesdales or Percherons, depending on your choice. They all had names. Kate and Harry, of course, because they were the names of our real horses, and Flick and Floss, Jack and Lady. The names of horses in a team had a fine euphony. I had a great stable of stick-horses when I was five.

You drove your stick-horses by clutching them at the top and digging them into the ground, in the same way as a mountain climber uses a staff. When the load was heavy, and the horses pulling hard, you dug in deep and shouted your head off – "Giddap, Kate! Come on, Harry boy, pullll! You can do it!" But with the drivers you just clicked your tongue, and away they went at a good slick trot down the dusty road.

Horses must have a stable, and the stable for my stick-horses was the rear outside wall of the garage that housed our Russell car. I'd marked off the stalls with little rows of stones, and each horse stood in his stall by simply leaning against the wall. It was necessary, horses being what they are, to pitchfork the manure from those stalls from time to time. I had a fork with a broken handle, and I'd work like a real farm-hand behind those horses, doing an essential job.

Unfortunately, my mentor in barn cleaning was a hired man who worked for us for a short time, named Nick Casey. Often I'd sit on the edge of the oat bin and listen to Nick shovel manure. And, horses being naturally ornery, he gave them many instructions in what was surely the most profane and colourful vocabulary in existence. "Move over there, you Roman-nosed bastard!" he'd command. "Stand still, you stupid bugger!" And these were just warm-ups for the really ripe stuff that followed. I stored all the words away in my head, to be used on my own steeds when they wouldn't behave.

Which brings me to that warm Saturday afternoon when I thought Dad was busy at the office. I was irritable and hot, just as Nick Casey usually was, and the stick-horses were at their orneriest. At the top of my piping voice I called them all the words I'd ever heard Nick use, along with some I'd picked up from my older brothers and a few that I invented. The air was blue.

Now it happened that Dad, whose strongest expletive ever was "Oh pshaw", had come home early from the office and was tinkering with the Russell inside the garage. The walls were thin, and my voice came through loud and clear. His reaction was immediate and positive. He didn't ponder as to whether or not he should ignore the incident. He didn't decide to write a letter to any friendly adviser in the newspaper, to ask what should be done about a swearing child. Nor did he consider taking me to a child psychologist. None of those things. What he heard was sinful, and he knew all about how to stop sinful actions in his children. He came around the corner of that garage with blood in his eye. He grabbed my best driving-horse, a lean and limber steed named Racer, and lambasted the tar out of me. I would like to be able to report that this licking cured me of swearing once and for all. But of course it didn't. I'm still a terrible curser. Similarly, my father never drank or smoked: most of his kids do. He went to church every Sunday of his life except when he was sick: most of his kids don't. So much for good parental example, and the power of the rod.

Such were the Nokomis days, the good days, the prosperous days when we lived in the biggest house in town, owned the first six-cylinder car in the district, and went for vacations to Watrous Lake. Father was the mayor of the town, and the president of the curling club, and the founder of the local chapter of the masonic lodge. No wonder the house and the yard, the horses, cats, dogs, chickens, and cows all stand out in my memory. But mostly I remember the people who lived in the old stone house with me – and what a wacky bunch they were!

2 *The Brothers and Sisters*

I always think of the brothers and sisters in pairs. As I knelt in my long flannelette nightie on the cold floor of the attic bedroom I shared with Hub I prayed for their blessing in groups of two. It was, "God bless Poppa and Momma". The essential pair. If anything happened to them I was done for, I knew. They alone stood between me and the moaning wind and the darkness and all the terrors of the night.

Then it was, "God bless Morley and Peter", the two oldest brothers, always referred to in our family as "the boys". Born just over a year apart, they played and fought and worked together constantly. They slept together, too, and sometimes when there was company or – later – a roomer, one of us younger kids would have to sleep with them – three in a bed. (This was a horror that I will deal with later.) They used to talk a lot in bed those two. I can still hear the soft rumble of their voices late at night or on a Sunday morning, "The way I figure it . . . if a fellow can only. . . ." Constantly, they would be trying to solve some intricate riddle of life.

Morley was lean, sharp-faced and wiry, with the reddest hair I've ever seen. He was a mild boy, quiet, good-natured and friendly, but with a keen sense of justice and a fiery temper. It didn't do to get him riled, as I once discovered when I foolishly recited in his presence the bit of doggerel, "Red-headed gingerbread . . . five cents a cabbage-head". He happened to be washing his hands at the time and they were covered with lather of strong soap and barn dirt. He simply turned and rubbed the grimy mess hard into my face until I howled for mercy.

As the oldest boy, one of Morley's chores was to dress me in the morning, and he hated it. As often as not he'd beat it and leave me to fend for myself, but he was always caught out because I invariably put my shoes on the wrong feet. Things of simple logic, such as which shoe goes on which foot, have always baffled me. If there's a wrong way to do it, I will.

Morley never managed to establish any real rapport with the Nokomis educational establishment. He hated to be cooped up in school, much preferring the fields, the dark brown soil, and the company of animals. About all I remember of his scholastic career is that he once threw a snowball at the principal and scored a direct hit, and that he left school early to work on the farm.

Doris and Phyllis, the next pair for whom I requested divine blessing, were also opposites. Doris had long black hair, and Phyllis's was red as a sunset. Doris was cautious, nervous; Phyllis active, saucy and adventuresome. They slept together, and hated it. Their arguments and accusations rang through the house.

"You're on my side of the bed again."

"I am not! It's just as much my side as it is yours!"

"Ha! If we drew a line down the centre . . . see . . . it would go right here."

"It would not."

"It would so. And your big b-t-end is at least a foot over it. Move it. . . ."

"It's no bigger than yours. . . ."

And so on – far into the night.

Hubert and Max were the next pair in the rhythm of the prayer. Hub. What can I say about Hub? His full name was Hubert Frances Warner, but you'd better stand well back if you intend to call him by his middle name. He was convinced that it was a girl's name, and nobody was going to call him that.

There used to be a magazine series entitled, "The Most Remarkable Character I've Ever Known" or something like that. Hub will always be my most remarkable character. Somehow his commonsense and toughness typify for me the early West. He just couldn't be licked. The school system attempted in its self-righteous stupidity to destroy him. It wasn't that he was rebellious or delinquent or mean. He'd have been delighted to fit into their neat little pattern, but they wouldn't let him. For Hub had been born with an almost complete inability to spell. None of the family spells well, but he was hopeless. He had a natural curiosity, and liked all the other school subjects. He could also remember how to put together the most complicated gadget after he'd taken it apart, and knew more stories than any other kid in the neighbourhood, as well as the location of every garden in town that had ripe tomatoes or carrots worth taking. But somehow that peculiar arrangement of nerve-ends, or whatever it is that makes some people good spellers, was lacking in his brain. The teachers looked upon this as a mean, deliberate attack on their status and security. *They* could all spell well, and anybody who couldn't must be bad.

So they told him he was no good and would never amount to anything; that he was a menace to himself and society, and would surely end up in jail. Hub simply didn't believe them. They must, he concluded, be nuts, to take such a ridiculous attitude and, since they were nuts, nothing they said had any relevance. He ignored them, and it's a good thing he did.

In contrast to Hub I tended to fit neatly into the school

establishment, and it's a good thing I did, for I had none of his practical ability. To his credit, he never held it against me, even when I left him far behind, and showed little malice even when Mother would demand, "Why can't you be more like Max? He never plays hookey." Despite her other admirable qualities, our mother was singularly lacking in tact.

An aunt who visited us when I was very small tells of coming upon me sitting in a round tin tub in the middle of the kitchen floor being bathed. And swearing and howling. Soap was getting into my eyes and mouth and ears, and while I squirmed and fought to get free of Doris, who was doing the job, I exploded with the ultimate in rage, frustration and scorn, "You . . . you . . . dirty Timothy Eaton coward!"

I've never been able to figure how old Tim should be connected with cowardice, but the mention of Eatons was natural enough, because their mail-order catalogue was the most important book in our household.

It had everything. A child could pore over it for hours, the way he might sit in front of a television set today, being amused, educated and mesmerized. Consider what that book had to offer. It brought us a whiff of the outside world, showing us how the other half lived. Ladies in fashionable clothes, riding in grand buggies, pulled by elegant horses. Sail-boats skimming along the margin of a lake. And, as today's boys sit dry-mouthed ogling television ads featuring semi-nude females, we could get our kicks from the women's underwear pages.

I think I liked the harness ads best. Great powerful white steeds with bulging muscles stood straining against the traces. There was an ad for a stump-puller, I remember, which showed a big horse walking in a circle. He was working a winch, which was attached to two monstrous stumps.

At any moment, one of them would be torn from the earth. To a boy who'd never seen a tree trunk thicker than a man's arm, these stumps, as big around as laundry tubs, were indeed a marvel.

For little girls, the catalogue was the perfect cut-out book, with children, adults, dolls, toys, furniture, baby carriages–everything they could want. On Valentine's day we cut out the faces of children and pasted them on bits of cardboard, along with red hearts and cute rhymes.

The catalogue was even used for shopping sometimes. Especially before Christmas, when we would lie on our bellies on the living room rug and pick out all the things we wanted but never got. Most of our clothing came from there, and there's never been a thrill like shoving your bare leg into the downy warmth of new fleece-lined drawers.

And when it was finished with in the house, the catalogue was moved to the toilet out back, where it performed an even more vital function. Nobody has yet got around to producing illustrated toilet paper–a frightful industrial oversight in my opinion–but when they do, it will not be better than the old Eaton's catalogue.

There was no partner for the last name in my prayers; it just sort of hung there like the last line in an unfinished couplet. "God bless Momma and Poppa . . . Morley and Peter . . . Doris and Phyllis . . . Denny and . . . uh. . . ." He was the youngest of the Nokomis family (Betty was born later in Prince Albert) and he was small and thin and red-headed and thoughtful. He suffered greatly from being the only one lower than me in the pecking order and I teased him without mercy. I knew exactly how to make him cry or swear, or laugh until he peed his pants. I could make him lose his temper completely, and he would fly into such a towering rage that he'd grab a butcher knife and chase me around the yard with it.

Why did I do this? I really don't know. Barbarism of children, I guess. I got it from above, so I dished it out below. He was my very own patsy, my meat. He was there, and I could handle him. What I did to him in those early days, the frustrations and rages and sorrows I caused, are as much built into his character as the effects of the bullying I got from above are built into mine.

So there we were. Seven new kids in a new town. In a country too young to have traditions of its own, making do with the religious and racial traditions brought in by that astonishing mixture of peoples. And what of us kids? Unknown to our parents–to ourselves, even–we developed new ways. Ways fashioned by the flat prairies, the black soil, the constant winds, the bone-dry summers and the mean winters. Fashioned, too, by the one-crop economy. A fatalism, an acceptance of what nature gave us. If it rained we were prosperous; if it didn't we were poor. Not just the farmers, but everybody else who worked for them. And no one could affect the amount of rainfall by a single drop.

A new race of Canadians we were. Not the fur traders or the Métis, but the solid dirt farmer. All the fatalism, sardonic humour, wildness, stubbornness–or strength of character, whichever you prefer–yes, and paranoia, too, all these began in Nokomis, and towns like it, with the Braithwaites and families like them. This country made us, and wherever we go and whatever we do, we can't ever be quite the same as other Canadians.

3 *Fire—Robbery—and the Beating of a Tender Heart*

Tiny waifs of memory loiter in my mind from those early Nokomis days. Why do they linger, when so many other things, which were probably of more importance, have been forgotten? Perhaps because they were big, like the first moving picture, a fire or a death. Or traumatic, scarring my little id with frustration, fear or rage.

There was the Great Christmas Fire, for instance. Beside threatening us with the loss of our home, it showed our family in all its madness. Christmas was big in our family. Not so much the religious connotation, except for a desultory concert in the Methodist church, but rather a Dickens-type Christmas. There were stockings carefully hung by the chimney, oranges that came but once a year, visitings, and the wonderful red and green decorations.

These decorations, very inflammable, were made of crêpe paper, and were stretched across the living room, looping down from the centre lamp, and tacked firmly in the corners. And huge red paper bells, which were stored flat, were opened up miraculously at Christmas to be hung in doorways and bump on people's heads.

At the time of the Great Fire, it may have been 1917 for all I know, the pre-Christmas scene was as follows: Warner Braithwaite, resplendent in shirt sleeves held in place by little metal garters, and a starched collar, stood sweating on a kitchen chair in the middle of the living room, the other furniture having been pushed back for the occasion. He was attaching streamers to the base of the lamp. This was a gas lamp, you must understand, and it was throwing a festive glow on the proceedings below.

Which proceedings consisted of the two young Braithwaites fighting over who was going to hold the streamers for Father, the two Braithwaite girls fighting over who would hand Mother the tinsel to be hung on the streamers, the five-year-old Braithwaite (me) trying to take a piece of candy from the baby (Denny), thus causing him to howl like a coyote. A normal, pleasant, domestic scene.

Suddenly the tranquility of the household was shattered by a loud scream from one of the girls. "The streamers are on fire!" And sure enough, this was indeed the case, for the heat from the gas lamp having ignited the paper, flames were dancing merrily as elves along the strings towards the fluffy living room curtains.

Then did pandemonium break loose. Everybody dropped what they were doing and ran. The little ones ran in circles, screaming, while the boys dashed out of the back door to the pump to fetch water. It took but a matter of minutes for Morley to prime the pump, fill a pail and dash through the door, leaving a trail of splashes, and pitch it all over the rug.

Hub was close behind and he had two buckets of water, one in each hand. "Clear the way for the Nokomis fire department!" he yelled, and his feet hit the icy water dropped by Morley. His feet went high above his head and so did the two buckets of water. Water covered everything – the kitchen cabinet, the curtains, and the surface of the large coal and wood range, sending a cloud of hissing steam up into the room.

At this point, Mother stuck her head into the cloud and asked, quite logically, "Hub, whatever did you do that for?" But Hub was gone for more water.

Doris, in the meantime, had dashed out of the front door and down the snow-covered street, her dark hair streaming in the wind, shouting, "My piano! Save my piano!" (Although both the boys had been subjected to piano lessons they'd never learned much, and Doris was the only who could play. So she looked upon the big, stolid upright piano as her personal property.)

The fire? Oh, Warner and Mary had pulled down the streamers and stamped them out with their feet. The only real damage was done by the water.

The next tiny tidbit of memory has to do with the Great Robbery. Since I was spectacularly involved in this, I'm well-acquainted with all of the details. It was the sort of thing that might well start a lad off on a career of crime, and often when the mood is on me I brood about this and consider how I might well have ended up on the gallows.

Across the lane from our house lived a retired gentleman by the name of Stickells. He was badly crippled up with rheumatism and so naturally everybody called him "Old Stiffy Stickells". Despite his stiffness, Mr. Stickells was an excellent runner, as I found out to my sorrow. He had a first-rate garden, and one lazy fall afternoon my big brothers, all three of them, were lazing about on our lawn, sucking on grass stems and wondering what to do. Finally, one of them suggested idly that I sneak into Stiffy's garden and fetch out some tomatoes that should be just about ripe by this time.

"But he's working in the other side of the garden," I protested.

"That doesn't matter," another said. "Everybody knows he's deaf and half-blind."

"Besides," Hub added, "he can't run. Even if he does see you he can't catch you."

It was a tradition in our family to send the youngest member to do any dirty work that was to be done. I looked around for Denny, but he was nowhere in sight, so I had to go.

My first foray was successful. I sneaked through the gate and into the tomato patch and Old Stiffy never so much as raised his head. But my small hands could carry only four ripe tomatoes and so I was soon sent back for more. The next time, though, Stiffy wasn't at his accustomed place and, when I looked over a row of tall beans, there he was coming down the path with two empty water pails to get water from our pump. I squirched down in the tomatoes, afraid to breathe, but just as he got opposite me Stiffy made a surprisingly quick dodge in my direction.

I got out of there as fast I could go, with Stiffy after me in full stride and our dog, Patsy, always on the alert for anything on the run, after him, yapping angrily at his heels. I circled the house at full tilt, and flew across the empty lawn but Stiffy was still gaining. He would have caught me, too, if the back door hadn't opened and Mother, attracted by Patsy's yapping, hadn't come out. We all stopped.

"Gracious, Mr. Stickells, don't you think you are too old to play tag with the children?" she remonstrated mildly. Stiffy was too dumbfounded and out of breath to comment. He staggered to the pump, got his water and staggered home, with Patsy still yapping at his heels.

Patsy must have joined our family before I did, because I can't remember a time when he wasn't there. I think he must have been Mother's dog. Like all the dogs we've ever had, it was impossible to definitely designate his breed. When asked what kind of a dog he was, Mother would say,

"Well . . . he's a small dog." If pressed further, she'd amplify, "A small black dog."

And indeed he was very small and very black. His hair was long and completely covered his face. All you could see when you looked at him was a pair of very red malicious eyes, and a tiny pink tongue when he was panting. He had no tail that anyone could ever see, and when he was standing up, not moving, it was impossible to tell which end was which.

Pound for pound, Patsy must have been the noisiest, cussedest and meanest little dog that ever lived. The only water pump in our end of town stood about twenty feet from our back door so that it was much more convenient for the neighbours to get their water from it than from the town pump six blocks away.

More convenient, but not easier. Patsy believed strongly in the sanctity of private property and would attack anyone who tried to get away with any of our water. In winter, as will happen with water in thirty-below weather, the accumulated splashings from the spout froze around the pump, making a mound of glare-ice. To fight your way up and down its slopes with two water-pails in hand, and Patsy tugging at your pantleg, was more than most of our neighbours could manage, and so they walked the six blocks to the town pump.

But of all the people who hated Patsy–and there were many–I think my sister Doris hated him worst. Doris had been bitten by a dog once. It was a family legend and was told over and over again. According to the story, this big dog had just come up and bitten her when she was crossing a field on the way to school, and Dad had been so enraged that he'd borrowed a gun and gone out and shot the animal, even though he'd never before shot anything in his life. This experience may have been the basis for Doris's dislike of canines, or it could be that she just didn't like the noise and the smell and the dirt they provided. At any rate, whenever anything untoward happened involving Patsy–which was about twice a day on the average–she would say with more scorn than I've heard anyone else achieve "And then they say – keep a dog!"

Doris was delicate in the Nokomis days. At least, she thought she was. Her most common affliction was a beating heart. Not one that was beating too little, but one that was beating too much. When Mother and Dad were away at the curling rink, as they were almost every night in the winter, they would be called off the ice to the phone to hear Doris's plaintive complaint, "Mother, my heart is beating again."

Whereupon Hub and I, for whom she was baby-sitting at the time, would dance around her chanting in asinine falsettos, "Mother, oh Mother, come home to me now, for my heart is beating again." This didn't help her condition any.

Actually, Doris was probably the most normal member of the entire family, and the most logical. Always interested in her health–well perhaps "interested" is too mild a word, "obsessed" would cover it better–she naturally became preoccupied with different nutrient values of foods. Indeed, after she became a teacher, nutrition was her major hobby. When she came home for Easter and Christmas holidays, she would be appalled to find that we were still eating potatoes and meat and bread. Especially white bread. It was, she had come to believe, thoroughly bad for you. She would say, "Well, if you persist in eating that white bread, you'll die some day." And if that isn't logic, what is?

While we lived in Nokomis we had periodic visits from Dad's Ontario relatives. They were all nice, pleasant, conservative people, and I suppose they wondered what kind of a crazy place Warner had got to. But the railways were providing good service by then, and the thing to do was for everyone to travel west to see the wonderful Rocky Mountains. Nokomis was in a sense on the route to the Rockies, so everyone would stop off for a week or two.

The visitor I remember best was Aunt Grace, who had had a hard time on an Ontario farm, and whose husband was dead. I don't know if she was an honest-to-god aunt or not – it was difficult to get all the exact relationships straight – but she was always called "Aunt Grace". The two things I liked most about her were that she could recite all the poems of Robert Service, and she walked in her sleep.

I don't think there was any relation between these two activities, but then there may have been. We kids would sit on the floor in the parlour while Aunt Grace sat in a rocking chair, going gently back and forth in time with the rhythm of the poem. As the action increased, so did her speed of rocking.

Thus, in "The Shooting of Dan McGrew" she would begin nice and slowly, then build up to such a pitch that by the time Dan was "pitched on his head and pumped full of lead" she was going at so great a rate that she nearly took off. I don't know which fascinated us most, the rocking or the poems.

More spectacular even than this furious rocking was the sleep-walking. It always followed the same pattern. Aunt Grace would have this dream, and would shout in a piercing scream "All out!" Then she would get out of bed, still asleep, light the coal-oil lamp, gather up all the bed-covers under one arm and, with the lamp in the other, would start through the house. Her route was always the same. She'd go down the hallway and through each of the bedrooms in turn, shouting "All out!" in each room. Whereupon each occupant would get up and follow her. Thus the night-shirt procession progressed from room to room, with Dad as close to Aunt Grace as he could get.

We'd all been well-briefed on the dangers of violently waking a sleep-walker. It might lead to sudden death, or worse. So nobody made a sound, although in winter our feet would get mighty cold, and the draft whistling up under our nighties was uncomfortable.

When she reached the head of the stairs, Aunt Grace would stop while we all held our breath. Then she would raise her hands high above her head, one holding the bed-clothes and the other the lamp, shout "Gone!" and hurl the bed-clothes down the stairs. This was my father's cue to step nimbly forward and grab the lamp. He could never feel certain she wouldn't pitch with the wrong hand.

Life was never dull when Aunt Grace came to live with us.

Nokomis was a very religious town. Although there were less than four hundred people altogether, there was a Methodist Church, a Presbyterian Church, a Baptist Church, a German Lutheran Church, a Roman Catholic Church, and, of course, an Anglican Church.

We were Methodists, which meant that we were the best people in town. We knew that the Catholics were evil (as did all good Northern Irish people); that the Anglicans were stuck up and hypocrites; that the Presbyterians were stubborn and mean. As for the German Lutherans, well! Germans! Everybody knew what they were jabbering about in their own language during the war. They were jabbering about the take-over of the country. No, you couldn't really trust anyone except the Methodists.

The Methodist Church was a small white one in the middle of town. I remember it well, for it was there that I had the three most traumatic experiences of my early years: I saw my first dead person; I saw my first movie; and I was lied to, horribly and deliberately, which led to my kicking the Sunday School superintendent in the shins.

The funeral was that of a neighbour, one of the founders of Nokomis. I was dragged along with the other members of the family to show our respect. I didn't want to go. I yelled and shouted that I didn't want to see a dead person, until I was informed that to take such an attitude was wicked, and would quite likely bar the gates of heaven against me. Well, I wasn't taking any chances like that, so I went.

I had seen the deceased before, of course, many times. She was very old and very wrinkled and very deaf. Often she would be brought over to our yard in the hot summer days, to sit in the shade of the box-elder trees. And we would be warned not to yell or shout or make a noise because it would disturb Grandma Pierce. Although why a noise should bother a stone-deaf person confused me.

And now she was dead. I'd seen dead cats, gophers, mice, even a dead horse once. It had fallen by the curb of the sidewalk downtown and broken its leg. It had to be shot on the spot, and while it lay there waiting to be hauled off we little kids took turns jumping over its outstretched head. As we did so the eye seemed to wink at us. But I'd never, ever seen a dead person.

So, clutching Dad's hand I was led up to the body. There she was, lying among all the flowers in her best dress. But she wasn't old any more. Gone were the wrinkles. Cheeks that had been hollow were plump and rosy, as they must have been when she was a young girl – before the pioneering, before the ten children, before the work, work, work of a Saskatchewan farm. Even her hair had been tinted and combed and made pretty. I stared and stared until Dad nudged me and whispered, "What's the matter, Son?"

"Why is she so pretty?" I gasped.

"Because she's happy. She's with God in heaven."

He believed it too, I'm sure he did. And I wish that I,

too, could believe that he himself became young again when he died, with all the lines of sorrow and bad luck and disappointment and work wiped away. And that with Mother, also made young again, he is happy somewhere. But I can't.

The movie. I've since heard it described as one of the great movies of all times, a "high point in the history of American movies". Certainly its advance publicity in Nokomis must have been thorough. Everybody talked about it. Why, it had even been shown in the White House to the President of the United States. It surely must have strong religious overtones, too, since it was to be shown in a Methodist church, and parents were encouraged to bring their children. It was called *The Birth of a Nation*.

The church was packed, with many people standing at the back. A huge screen had been erected across the front and, when the lights were put out and the titles flickered across the screen, a sigh of anticipation escaped from the lips of the crowd. A moving picture! A story right there before their eyes! Certainly it had all the ingredients to make it great: all sorts of killing and violence, racial hatred, vigilantes riding in white robes and – sex. Ah yes, raw sex. At the scene where the giant Negro picks up the squirming white girl, with her long blonde tresses falling in disarray, you could feel the rut in that good Methodist church. As for me, I was scared stiff.

Afterwards, the whole country talked of little else but the wonder of the film. The Methodist minister preached a sermon on "The role of the moving picture in spreading Christ's word." The Lutheran minister said it was "the work of the devil". The *Nokomis Times* ran an editorial assessing the prospects of making Nokomis the movie capital of Canada.

My third bad experience in that little white Methodist church sowed the first seeds that were to eventually turn me off churches entirely. We, of course, went to Sunday School. Mother firmly believed that Sunday School training was the best possible thing for her children. She never once stopped to wonder if perhaps the Sunday School teachers, untrained, untested, often uneducated, might also be lesbians, homosexuals, bigots, or fools. The fact that they did their work in the church made them perfect in her eyes.

Well, our superintendent certainly wasn't perfect. At worst he was a sadist; at best a liar. His name was Mr. Watcherling. He liked to tell the little kids what would happen to them if they were bad. They would go to hell and burn forever. Watcherling's eyes would shine when he said this. "Have you any idea what 'forever' means, young man? Not just a day–or a week–or a year, but year after year after year–forever! Red hot pokers shoved through your flesh, birds pecking out your eyes–forever!" And since being bad included, I was sure, stealing apples, teasing your little brother, badgering Stiffy Stickells, I was obviously for it. That is, I would have been if I'd believed him, but of course I didn't. I've often wished there were a hell, though, just so that Mr. Watcherling could go there.

His biggest and meanest lie was the one about Santa Claus. My parents, of course, did the Santa Claus bit just as all good, God-fearing parents thought they must. But they never overdid it. If you asked pointed questions they'd hedge or walk away. Not good old Watcherling, however. To him Santa was one of God's agents, who could mete out minor and more immediate favours and punishments.

As the jolly season drew nearer, Watcherling grew more vicious. "Don't forget, young gentlemen, Santa Claus is coming right to this church. He'll come right through that door there with his pack on his back, and there'll be presents for the children who have been good, and none for those who have been bad!"

On the strength of that I became good. I memorized a whole long poem for the Christmas concert. It was titled "Just Before Christmas" and each verse ended with the line "So, jest 'fore Christmas I'm as good as I can be." I did all the things advocated in the poem. I said "yessum" to the ladies and "yessir" to the men, and when there was company, I didn't pass my plate for pie again. I washed my face and brushed my teeth and minded my "p's and q's". And I didn't bust out my pantaloons, and I didn't wear out my shoes. I was so good, in fact, that Mother thought I was sick.

So, on the evening of the concert I said my piece, requiring prompting only four times. Then I sat on the edge of my chair, waiting for that old whiskered rascal to show up. Finally, after interminable telegrams detailing his progress from the North Pole, he did actually walk in through that back door – cotton whiskers, red suit, rubber boots, harness-bells and all. With a "Ho ho ho," he dumped his pack on the floor under the Christmas tree, and began to shout out names. I waited, scarcely breathing. I had my order in for a meccano set, and I knew that if there was any justice in the world at all, I'd get it.

The names were called off – Helen Rath, Alan Bird, Dwight Whitworth – down the line it went. The pile began to diminish. Hubert Braithwaite, Morley Braithwaite – all the rest of the family. Each kid came back to his seat grinning and shaking his parcel. There were tinker-toys, sleds, Parcheesi games and snakes-and-ladders. Still I waited, but my grin was getting a little forced. Finally the bag was empty, and my name had never been called. There were kids all around me who I knew had been little stinkers. And they'd got presents. How could I have been that bad? My shame and humiliation was complete.

Just as we were about to leave the church, Watcherling came smirking down the aisle to greet my parents. He stood in front of us and smiled toothily. I'm sure he didn't know I'd been left out. Then he placed his big sweaty hand on my tow head and said what he shouldn't have. "Didn't I tell you Santa would reward good little boys?" It was then I let him have it in the shins with my hard-toed boots.

Years later I learned that it had all come about because of a ridiculous mix-up between my parents – each thought the other was taking care of it. We had a jolly laugh about it then. But at the time they couldn't explain it to me, because the whole present thing was based on a lie – a cruel, needless lie.

There must be better ways of getting a six-year-old to be good.

4 *School*

I started school in the fall of 1918 and it was a disaster.

The Nokomis school stood on the edge of town and was a two-storey, frame building with two rooms upstairs and two downstairs. It was what they called a "continuation school", which meant that all the grades were there, from Grade One to as high as you wanted to go. I could see it across the field from my attic window, and I looked forward to that first day with terror.

Of course my older brothers had prepared me for the sacrifice.

"That Primary teacher is a holy terror," Morley said, frowning and shaking his head.

"She sure is," another smart alec added. "Got a strap in her desk drawer two feet long and four inches wide. We can hear the smack of it clear up in our room."

"And you'll have to watch yourself. Can't talk, can't leave the room without asking, can't do hardly anything."

Hub, who was already in Grade Three, but would be in the same room as myself, added his own bit of advice. "You'll have to watch that weak bladder of yours, or Miss Williams will kill you."

My weak bladder was a great embarrassment to me, and a great annoyance to Hub. We slept together and often, in the middle of the night as I lay cuddled against him spoon-fashion, I'd dream that I was outside peeing against a fence. Then I'd feel the scalding liquid on my thighs and belly and hear Hub's furious, "God damn it, Fat, you've done it again! Hey, Ma!" The shout would ring through the house, compounding my shame. "Fat's peed the bed again. I'm soaked!" It was a terrible affliction, and the more I tried to cure it the more nervous I got, and the more I peed the bed.

"Now stop that, you boys," Mother warned, "or I'll take a stick to you." She didn't want anything to interfere with getting me out of the house. She had Denny to look after, and it was much easier to do without me there. So she dressed me up in my best clothes – stiff, clumsy-laced boots, long black stockings held up with elastic garters, pants buckled at the knee, a clean jersey and a peaked cap on my head. I looked good enough to eat, she said.

The boys watched this with disgust. They were to take me to school, and hated the idea. As soon as we got outside into the crisp September sunshine and they got me started along the winding path that led across the field to school, they beat it as fast as they could go. I stumbled along through the pigweed and ripening goldenrod, bawling and swearing with rage and frustration. Then I tripped over a rut and fell, and tore the knee of my stocking. That did it. I galloped home, frightening the sparrows and blackbirds with my howls.

Mother had a small conference with the boys at noon, and so they dragged me off to school after lunch, and conveyed me as far as the schoolyard gate. There they left me, alone and frightened, watching the millions of screeching, chasing, squabbling kids that filled the yard. I was safe from bullying, though. Morley was one of the biggest kids in the school, and he saw to it that nobody messed with his little brother. He might badger me a bit himself – that was his privilege. But he wasn't about to let anyone else dare try it.

Finally the big bell in the cupola on the roof rang, and I followed that screeching mob into the school, leaving behind forever the carefree life. There were three grades in the Primary room and the beginners were on the outside row next the windows, sitting in double seats far too big for us. My seat-mate was a big, tousle-headed farm boy by the name of Rudolph Lampe, but everybody called him "Noodles". He wore overalls and immense boots, and drove to school in a buggy. He was ripe with the smell of horse.

The teacher was small and pretty, but that didn't fool me. I knew that her trim frame housed a demon. I tried to make myself invisible by squirching down in my seat but because I'd missed the morning indoctrination she singled me out.

"Will the new boy please stand and tell us his name."

I'd been rehearsed in this by my mother who insisted I give all my names. Mother had a thing about names; each of her eight children were endowed with three, making a total of some twenty-four in all. She loved the sound of names, making sure that each combination had a good ring to it.

But I hated mine. Why couldn't I have one simple one like other kids – Bill, or Pete, or Alan.

"Come on," she urged. "Don't be shy. Tell us your name."

So I stood up and shouted defiantly for all the world to hear – "John Victor Maxwell Braithwaite!" My gawd, what a handle! Even now it embarrasses me to say it. There was a loud guffaw from the back seat of the last row on the other side of the room, where Hub sat with a noisy cohort. "We all call him Fat," he apologized to the class. And from that time forward all the rest of them did, too.

The teacher gave me a slate and some little wooden bright-coloured pegs and a round stick of plasticine, with an Eddy's match box to keep it in, and a piece of tattered oilcloth to protect the scurfy surface of the desk, and a green primer with pictures of apples in it. She then left us to our own devices, while she tried to teach some reading to the Grade Threes.

Soon I began to get that familiar feeling. I was being too soon cooped up. The natural thing for me to do was to step behind the barn or into the trees, or just let it go. But now I needed permission, and permission was hard to get.

The harassed teacher was busy at the other side of the room and, for some reason, there had been a raft of hand-raising on our side. There were the snappers who, with a quick twist of the wrist, could bring their fingers together with a loud crack. There were the puffers who heaved and gasped as they waved their hands, like a steam locomotive on a grade. There were the jumpers who leaped half out of their seats as their hands shot up. And then there was me who, with my dread of drawing attention, would raise my hand tentatively, then jerk it down again when I saw the teacher look my way.

So it was that by the time I got Miss Williams' attention my need was monumental and her patience was gone.

"Well?" she snapped.

"Please may I leave the room?"

"I said no one else can leave the room. It's almost recess time."

The next time my hand went up more frantically.

"No, I told you . . . no more leaving the room."

"But. . . ."

It was no use. She wouldn't even look. Then up went the hand of big, quiet, stolid Noodles.

"I suppose," the teacher barked, "that you want to leave the room, too."

"Please no." He had moved over so far to his side that

another inch would have put him on the floor. He pointed to the seat between us . . . where an amber puddle was spreading closer and closer to him. "I want that Max should leave the room."

School had its compensations, though. I soon discovered that I was pretty quick to learn, and this gave me status. I was in a new pecking order now, not one governed by age or sex or rotundity, but by ability. It was good to get praised by the teacher and get little stars pasted on my slate for getting my number work right. I could memorize like the mischief and, since much of our learning was by rote, it gave me little trouble. "Tom Tinker has a dog. Tom Tinker said: 'I love my dog and my dog loves me. I fed my dog under a hollow tree. My dog says bow-wow.' " "Betty Pringle had a cat. Betty Pringle said. . . ." But why go on? I'm sure I've demonstrated my superiority.

Besides, I came to love Miss Williams. She was so pretty and she moved so gracefully and pouted her mouth so bewitchingly when she leaned close to me to inspect the work on my slate. I'd have died for Miss Williams. In my fantasies I was forever rescuing her from ruffians, and being hurt, and smiling bravely without complaint.

She was one of the few teachers who understood Hub's lack of spelling ability. Oh it annoyed and bewildered her, but she didn't berate or humiliate him. It wasn't until we moved to Prince Albert that the teachers began their concerted efforts to destroy him.

It was also in Grade One that the little serpent of sex began to stir. It was directed towards Marion Murphy who sat in the seat ahead, and whose long, dark curls draped over my desk. Did I dare to touch her, to feel her softness?

Of course I couldn't play with Marion at recess, because the boys were restricted to one side of the school playground, and the girls to the other. But I enticed her into our big yard at home, and here she came with flashing eyes and dimpled smile. Oh the soft firm arms, and the girl smell. The eternal female, coaxing yet distant, coy, mysterious, frustrating, exciting. I taught her the games that small boys teach small girls. We built our house in the currant bushes, far from prying eyes, and taught each other the innocent secrets of life.

The idyll ended, though, when I got her into trouble. It was the scandal of the neighbourhood, and her parents forbade her to ever come into our yard again.

It was once more my stomach that got me into the trouble, and my passion for apples. Each autumn, big round barrels of apples arrived from Dad's district in Ontario. What a harvest! There was a barrel of cooking apples and a barrel of eating apples. I favoured the cooking apples for the obvious reason that they were bigger. They were harder, too, of course, but my appetite ran to quantity rather than quality.

Since there were so many of us, and since Mother liked to have a few apples left for pies, and to polish up for Christmas, she was forced to limit the family to one apple each a day. I don't know how the others stood it, but one apple a day was just an aggravation to me. And so it was my practice to sneak into the cellar where they were stored and steal them.

To accomplish this, I used the coal chute, a square wooden attachment which led into the dark, damp cellar, and down which the big lumps of Alberta coal were slid to be burned in the furnace. I would pry off the lid of the coal chute, slide down, land with a thump on the pile of coal, and then find my way, by smell mostly, to the apple barrels.

As the level of apples went down in the barrel, the more difficult it was for me to get them out. I'd reach as far as I could over the rim and sometimes my feet would completely leave the floor. But oh! the smell! Like all the apple orchards in the world condensed into one small space. I would feel around in that pungent darkness until I got hold of the biggest apple and then squirm my way out again, up through the coal chute and into the barn, or some such secluded place, to munch on it. Heaven.

Well, one day in late November when we already had winter clothes on, I figured that I'd pressed my luck a little far, and maybe a substitute thief would do the job better. So, by whatever means children use to con other children into doing their dirty work, I persuaded Marion to go down the coal chute for me. This was fine, except that she happened to be dressed in a brand new red overcoat, with buttoned leggings to match, and a new red bonnet. It was very cute, until she started down that coal chute. Then she noticed what was happening to it and began to cry. I shouted down something about stop acting like a stupid girl and making so much racket.

This only brought on more racket, which was now rising to a scream. I reached down the coal chute to rescue her–caught hold of her hand and began to pull, but somehow she got stuck. A girl caught in a coal chute, I soon discovered, is just about noisier than a girl caught anywhere else. I could see that things were rapidly reaching a climax, and that any minute my mother would be heading for the cellar to catch the thief.

I panicked and lit out of there as fast as I could go.

After that, Marion Murphy rarely played "London Bridge is Falling Down" with me. In fact, she wouldn't play anything, and she designated me–when she talked to me at all–as "you nasty boy". So my first love affair was ended before it ever could be consummated.

My scholastic career was interrupted shortly after it began with the arrival of the terrible influenza. The disease began in the trenches, came home with the soldiers, and spread so quickly across Canada that many believed it was carried by the winds. Whole families were struck down, doctors worked themselves to death, men in the cities wore masks to ward off the malignant curse, housewives kept indoors and away from their neighbours.

Our entire family got it, including Dad's youngest brother, Victor, who had come west to make his fortune and was staying with us until something turned up. We were all in bed, laid so low that the town policeman, Constable McGraw, had to come and milk the cow, feed the hens, slop the pigs and kill chickens so that Mother could drag herself from bed and make broth for the rest of us.

The treatment was simple. Keep the fever down with aspirin and castor oil, and try to avoid the killing pneumonia that often followed. For some reason that nobody has ever been able to explain, the disease hit young adults the hardest, and carried off many a father or mother–or both–from growing families. Mother and Dad were the right age for destruction, but they were too tough. Their forebears had lived through the terrible plagues that killed thousands of Irish immigrants on their way to this country, and deep within them was the strength to fight the flu.

I remember my own bout of flu well. I was deathly sick, burning up with fever one moment, shuddering with terrible chills the next. The walls of the bedroom would draw far, far off, leaving me in the centre of a great hall, filled with strange and terrible echoes. Then they'd close in on top of me, rushing at me, squeezing my chest, strangling me, until I twisted and screamed, fighting for breath.

Old Doc Brown, father of young Doc Brown who'd fetched me, was pressed into service, as was many another retired doctor. I remember him sitting on the edge of my bed, an unfamiliar wrinkled-faced, white-haired figure, a bottle of castor oil in one hand (the cure for everything in our household) and an immense spoon, ten times as large as my mouth, in the other. And me lying there with my lips clamped shut and my eyes staring in terror.

"Come on, Max," he said. "Take this and the next time I come I'll bring you a bag of chocolates."

I took it (God, I can still taste the horror of it!) and he did bring the chocolates. Two weeks later, he was dead of pneumonia, brought on by the flu, which had been brought on by overwork. Many a good doctor died that winter from fatigue, and we hadn't any to spare.

That was the same year we burned the Kaiser in Nokomis–"Kaiser Bill went up the hill to take a look at France. Kaiser Bill came down the hill with a bullet in his pants." An effigy of the old rascal hung in the front of the harness-maker's store, beside a new set of harness and the pelt of an immense wolf that somebody had shot on the plains. Complete with moustache and peaked cap it was. Walking past it, and gazing upon it with my six-year-old eyes, I was never one hundred per cent sure whether it was a real man or not. And when, after the shooting had stopped, and the town was celebrating our "glorious victory", this effigy was burned on a great pile of lumber–I still wasn't sure.

The burning took place on a field beside the tennis court. (The lumber had been salvaged from the blowing-down of the skating rink.) I stood there, clutching Dad's hand, squinting against the brightness of the flames, and the black smoke curling up into the blacker night. And the flames licked up around the Kaiser's head and I was terrified for him.

"Papa, why are they burning him?" I asked.

"Because he was a wicked man. He started the war!"

Standing close to me, and also clutching his father's

hand, was my close friend Cyril Redpath. He's dead now; fell off a freight train years later while running away from the cops. What happened to him? I don't know. I only know that when I played with him in Nokomis we were equally culpable. Together we roamed the streets of Nokomis and the immediate countryside. Tagged after the bigger kids when they snared gophers and played run-sheep-run up and down the dark alleys at night. Watched them swimming in Shunkies, a ditch beside the railway track where the water stayed until late in July. All the white bodies diving in and out, plastering each other with mud, and ducking behind the stacked snow-fences, in order to hide their nakedness from passengers in the CNR *Transcontinental* as it roared by.

There is one adventure we had that I'll never forget, because it was the only time in my life that I had too much to eat. Cyril's father ran the general store down on Main Street. A wonderful place–with bins of cookies, jars of candies, barrels of crackers, and stacked bags of flour. There were dry goods there, too. Rubber boots and overalls and ladies' button shoes, and men's straw hats, I remember. And in the back, pungent-smelling harness hung on pegs.

Cyril and I were in there one Saturday morning, standing, eyes level with the top of the counter, watching the wonderful transactions. All that money. Unbelievable. And then it happened. A farmer put a five-dollar-bill down on the counter and, as an afterthought, asked for some dried beans. Harry Redpath turned and scooped them out of a bin into a paper bag while the farmer turned to examine work socks, leaving that five-dollar-bill unguarded. A small hand snaked out and back, and two small forms disappeared through the front door.

What a time we had! At the Chinese restaurant we blew the entire five dollars on candy. Liquorice plugs and pipes, black-balls, all-day suckers, candy kisses, gooey marshmallows, and–the crowning delight–a full, two-pound box of chocolates.

Clutching all this loot, we hurried across the tracks and in the shade of a grain elevator sat down and consumed the lot. Oh, the wonder of it! All the candy you could eat. Nobody to say, "You've had enough now"; no brother or sister to share it with. No thought of keeping some for the next day. Just gobble it up. And then, oh the belly-ache! A belly-ache that started in the stomach and spread all over the body. We rolled on the grass and groaned until our stomachs rebelled completely and heaved the whole gooey mess out. And what tasted so good going down was so foul on the return journey. Late that afternoon we staggered home, were dosed with castor oil, and put to bed. But nobody ever knew the real story of our wild bacchanal.

"Was the war bad?" I asked my father as we watched the Kaiser burn.

"Very bad. Many good men were killed in it."

"Why did they have it, then?"

"Oh–many reasons, I suppose. But they'll never have another. That was the last one. A war to end wars. It can't ever happen again."

It was in the spring of the next year that I saw my first aeroplane. It was recess, and we were playing pump-pump-pull-away in the school yard. Chasing each other, squealing, shoving, arguing. And then this sound. Like a motor-bike or an automobile (there were a few automobiles in Nokomis already) but, wonder of wonders, this was coming from above. Every kid stopped running and turned his bare face to the sky.

"Look!" one shouted. "Away, way up there. See? It's too big for a bird!"

"Don't be so stupid," an older kid scoffed. "It's an aeroplane. I've seen them in a magazine my Dad gets from the old country. They used them in the war to fight with."

"How does it stay up?" a little girl asked.

"With wings, of course, you dumb girl."

"Hey . . . look . . . it's circling around."

And sure enough it was. Making large circles in the sky and coming lower and lower towards a stubble field on the edge of town. Then it disappeared behind a strawstack.

"It's landing!" my big brother Morley shouted. "Come on!"

So we jumped the fence and headed for the stubble field. Every kid from Grade One to Grade Eight. That school yard emptied like a hog-yard at slopping time.

The four teachers followed as fast as they could run.

When we got there, running carefully in our bare feet through the prickly stubble, there was a big crowd of townspeople already gathered. The aeroplane, a two-seater B.E. 2C bi-plane, was roped off to protect it from inquisitive hands. The pilot, a lean young man in leather jacket, breeches and leather leggings, stood idly dangling his helmet and goggles in his hand while he talked to Floyd MacDougal, recognized by all to be the best mechanic in the country.

We kids from the school quickly penetrated the crowd, wormed our way out to the front, and stared at the man from the sky. A new breed. A new man. Imagine being up above the trees, the houses, even the grain elevators!

"How fast will it go?"

"Over a hundred miles an hour, I heard him say."

"A hundred miles an hour! Faster than Doc Harding's car!"

"Gosh!"

But the daring young man wasn't there just to amaze us with the wonders of his flying machine. He was there to make money. Discharged from the Royal Flying Corps, with only one marketable peacetime skill, he was "barnstorming" around the country, selling rides to the adventurous. "Five dollars for five minutes in the air . . . up in the clouds . . . if you've the nerve for it." You sat in the front cockpit with no cover of any kind, and only a strap to keep you from falling out.

Who would be the first to step forward and risk his neck?

Well, the first to step forward, much to our amazement, was our own Grade One teacher, Miss Williams. My six-year-old heart thumped right down onto the dusty stubble. There was no rescue I could perform. I couldn't even talk. The pilot helped her in and fastened the straps. Then he got in and signalled to Floyd MacDougal, who removed the blocks from in front of the two spindly wheels and spun the propeller. It caught, and the dust rose in a cloud as the crowd moved back a respectable distance, the men holding their hats against the wind and the women holding their skirts. I was holding my breath.

The roar and wind increased incredibly. The thin, wire-spoked wheels began to turn. The frail craft bumped across the uneven field. For a long time it rattled along the earth. Then, slowly it wobbled into the air while three-quarters of the population of Nokomis let out a rousing cheer. The wings shuddered a bit, but she stayed up, gradually gaining altitude. The pilot circled back and came in low over the crowd. We scattered and cheered and waved our caps like crazy.

The pilot stayed around for two days, taking people up for rides. The grown-ups of the town talked of little else for weeks. Jimmy Spence, who ran the drug store, said that the things would never be of any practical use. All right as a toy, maybe, but you'd never get *him* up in one. Harry Bruce at the livery stable scoffed at the whole idea. The horse, he said, would always be the principal means of transportation and power. Look at the motor-car. Completely undependable. Reverend Millar preached a sermon about it on the text–"No matter how high ye may fly, there is always a reckoning." And the Grade Eight teacher got back at his class for leaving the school yard by making them write a composition about "The future of the aeroplane."

As for us little kids, we played aeroplane endlessly. An orange crate makes a great fuselage, since it already has two seats. It doesn't take much work to fasten two long boards to the rear end, coming to a point where a couple of pieces of cardboard make a tail. On the front, an apple box with a board on a spike makes a first-class propeller. So we'd pull our imaginary goggles down over our eyes, adjust our imaginary helmets, shout "Contact!" and Brrrorrr, away we'd go into the wild blue yonder to shoot down the Huns by the dozen. An older kid had got hold of newspaper clippings that told about Billy Bishop and everybody wanted to be him. Baron von Richthofen–the bum–nobody wanted to be.

5 *Hallowe'en Horrors*

Hallowe'en night in Nokomis was a night of horrors. There was none of your dolling yourself up in Aunt Ellen's old dress and clumping up to front doors begging for treats. No, it was a night of vengeance. A night when the young took it out on the old, when revolution and protest and defiance and violence filled the air. A night of mystery, when adults crouched in their homes, not in fear of witches and black cats and ghosts, but of kids. And of the roaming, hell-raising bands of young men, And people prayed that the gangs would pass them by and not single them out for reprisal.

There was something of the old Celtic idea of the beginning of winter in our Hallowe'en nights. Certainly the first snow often came on October thirty-first, and that was the official end of autumn. Winter would lay hold of us after that, and end any roaming of streets at night.

It was the official end of hard work, too. Harvest was finally done. The grain and the gardens were all in. There were chores to do, of course, cows to milk, stock to feed, wood to cut and haul, but the big job of getting in the grain was over. "Bringing in the sheaves," they sang in the little white church. "We shall come rejoicing, bringing in the sheaves."

So the young men from the farms, transients who'd been working on the threshing gangs, regular hired men, and the wild young sons of farmers would come into town in buggies, or astride clumping work horses, to raise hell. The focal point for their fun was the Chinese café, for the Chink was always fair game.

The Chinese café was an institution of the prairies. Every town had one, and they all looked about the same. Narrow, dark places with a counter on one side and a row of shabby booths with wooden benches on the other. The benches were especially built so that it was impossible to sit comfortably on them. They had a tendency to slide the sitter under the table, so that he had to keep feet braced and elbows at the ready.

But the café was the only place to go for a cup of coffee or a meal, or to meet and gab with other farmers. "The Chinaman's", as it was called, took the place of the club, the pub, the recreation centre. Since there was officially no liquor at all in Saskatchewan then, the Chinaman often also became the local bootlegger, supplying a horrible brand of rotgut homebrew concocted in somebody's dirty cellar.

One might suppose that since the Chinaman performed such a variety of essential services he'd be treated with some kindness by the locals. Not a chance. Since the community comprised such a mixture of nationalities, racial prejudice was a luxury the pioneers couldn't afford. Except for the Chinaman. That bewildered individual was the outlet for all the pent up racial bigotry of the district. He was alone, helpless, beyond the pale. Even the kids could badger him without restraint:

Chinky chinky Chinaman,
Sitting on a rail.
Along came a blackbird
And snipped off his tail.

After that, the rhyme got dirtier and meaner, and we kids

never passed the Chinese café without chanting at least a part of it.

The Chinaman retaliated by serving the foulest meals ever tasted. He usually lived alone, because the laws of the land prevented him from bringing over his wife or children. He made his home in the tiny rooms behind or above his café where, by peeking in the windows, we'd catch glimpses of him poring over Chinese newspapers or eating with chopsticks.

We knew he was eating some loathsome mess known as "chop suey". Chop suey! The very name filled us with revulsion. We had some vague idea it contained chopped up rats or toads, or something equally horrible. We had no idea that the Chink was actually dining on savoury, succulent Chinese food, cooked with loving care, in dazzling contrast to the greasy mess he threw in front of the farm hands, travelling salesmen, section labourers and the rest of us. Fat bacon was our lot, and old eggs; tired, warmed-over potatoes, shrivelled peas that hadn't seen their tinny home in days, followed by "laisin pie", with a leather crust that no one ever ate, and coffee you couldn't believe.

There also persisted an unpleasant, murky notion that the evil Chinese were constantly on the look-out for sweet, innocent Christian girls whom they enticed into their dens and violated with their corkscrew penises. What other obscenities were committed in those small back rooms could only be imagined, and, believe me, we imagined plenty.

At one point, the official records show that gangs of toughs wrecked the Chinese café in Nokomis so regularly, and so thoroughly, that the harassed owner was finally forced to close the place and try his luck elsewhere.

But the best-remembered incident was what the rowdies did to a Chinaman named Charlie one Hallowe'en night. Charlie was a dapper young man who, like his white contemporaries, was anxious to get ahead in the community.

He was handsome, sleek-headed, always polite and soft-spoken, and laughed a lot, showing straight rows of beautiful white teeth. He obviously had some money behind him, because he fixed up the Chinese café so that it was better than it had ever been, the booths painted in attractive colours, and new linoleum on the floor.

In a effort to establish himself with his fellow businessmen, he treated them to a dinner. The menu, cooked by himself, consisted of chow mein, sweet and sour, fu yung, egg rolls and other Chinese delicacies. My father, strictly a meat-and-potatoes Methodist, conceded that it was actually pretty good when you got used to it, and that Charlie was "as decent a fellow as most white men he'd ever met." However, not one of the so-impressed businessmen even considered inviting Charlie to his home in return.

But Charlie made one terrible mistake. To brighten up his place, and improve the service, he hired as a waitress a handsome Swedish girl from one of the farms. Her name was Olga, and it was soon apparent from the way she and Charlie looked at each other behind the counter that their relationship was developing into much more than that of employer and employee.

The young bucks of the district, some of whom had made their own crude overtures to Olga, eyed this relationship with deep resentment. Imagine that filthy Chink with a white woman! *They'd* heard all the stories about Chinese and the white slave trade and they weren't, by gawd, going to permit anything like that in their community. Of course they couldn't do much about it but sulk, since Charlie had come to terms with the Establishment, but Hallowe'en now, that was a different matter.

They cursed and muttered darkly about tar and feathers. Probably that's all they would have done, had not the preacher chosen on the last Sunday of the month to talk about the origins of All Hallow's Eve, and how it was celebrated by the Celts with bonfires. Hey, that would do the trick. A bonfire! Boy, wouldn't that warm old Charlie's pants for him, eh? There was a lot of laughing and back slapping and yes-by-godding, we'll burn the yellow bastard's place down!

Then the obvious fact penetrated their thick skulls that if they put fire to Charlie's place the whole street of bone-dry frame buildings would go with it. There was no fire equipment in town, and when a blaze got going, and the wind caught it, that was the end. Many another town had been wiped out in just such a manner..

Then Harry Tompkins had an even better idea. Sitting on a table in his folk's living-room was a hand-grenade that had been brought home from the war. There it sat in wrinkled glory, and Harry had become something of a local hero by recounting how good he'd been at throwing these things, and how he'd wiped out more than one machine-gun nest. "Just pull that there little pin," he'd explain, "then throw the bugger fast because when she blows she'd blow this house higher'n a kite."

His listeners shuddered at the very thought of it. And gazed fascinated at the small pin.

"If we was to toss that little baby in through Charlie's window," Harry told his pals over a jug of home-brew in the livery barn, "it might blow some sense into that horny Chink."

So the plans were laid, and late, late on Hallowe'en night a dozen or so of the bravest young men gathered in the vacant lot behind Charlie's. Down amidst the drying pigweed and tin cans and broken bottles they crouched, waiting, and sucking courage from the homebrew bottle. Finally Olga left for the night, the lights went out and all was quiet.

What happened next was subsequently re-told so often that the details, in fact the very dialogue, were well-documented.

Harry Tompkins fished into his pocket and pulled out the wicked little oval of iron. Again he explained how the thing was worked. "Just pull this little pin here and count three, then let her go, right through Charlie's window."

Nobody laughed now, and somebody suggested that the treatment was a little drastic.

"What the hell, he's only a Chink!"

Of course. That settled it.

"Don't forget to count three," Harry admonished.

"Ain't you going to do it?" somebody asked.

"Well . . . shit . . . I supplied the grenade. I can't do everything in this frigging deal. Besides, my throwing arm's a bit stiff."

More silence then. Who would toss the grenade? The effects of the homebrew were wearing off, and here they were. Couldn't just pack up and go home. Not after so much talk and all. Besides, who would suggest such a thing? Charlie's building loomed a black mass in the darkness. They knew it was there, and they knew something had to be done about it. The night was bitter cold and snowflakes whirled by in the wind. The gang shuddered collectively.

At this point I suppose they might have left, gone and shoved over a few outhouses, maybe burned up a shed, and then gone home. But suddenly Charlie's bedroom light went on again. Through the drawn window blind they could see his shadow moving about. Then the back door creaked open and the pale waving light of a lantern showed, as Charlie started down the path towards his own backhouse.

"He's going for a shit," one of them whispered. "Now's our chance."

"Yeah, throw the goddamn grenade," another admonished. "While he's not in there. After all, we don't want to kill the bugger."

It was the perfect solution. With half-frozen fingers

Harry fumbled with his grenade. "Got to find the bloody pin," he mumbled drunkenly. Then–"Ah . . . that's it."

"Let 'er go, Nute!" one of the gang yelled, but Harry didn't let her go.

"What's happened?"

"I dropped the goddamned thing . . . in the weeds . . . help me find it!"

"No . . . no . . . get the hell out of here . . . fast!"

But they weren't quite fast enough. They had scarcely stumbled and scrambled and rolled a dozen yards before the frosty air was split by the damnedest explosion Nokomis had ever heard. No one was actually killed, but the next day Doc Brown had to dig a few splinters of shrapnel out of a few backsides. Nobody bothered Charlie much after that.

It was to the younger boys, between the ages of eight and fifteen, however, that Hallowe'en night really belonged. All year long they kept an unofficial record of people of the town, some of whom would be left relatively alone, and others who would "get it". Before the actual night, kids spent hours preparing tic-tacs, a fiendish device made by notching the edges of the biggest spool you could find, putting a spike through the hole, and wrapping a string around the spool. When the notched edges were held tight against a window and the string yanked hard, spinning the spool on the spike, the resulting racket had been known to make old ladies jump clear out of their rockers.

Then gates were noted for lifting, and old buggies or waggons that could be taken apart and put up on somebody's veranda roof. Wood-piles to be pushed over, garden gates to be hung on telephone poles. No real damage, just something to make adults work the next day, and to remind them that kids weren't altogether helpless.

The thing that made Hallowe'en night worthwhile, however, were the little buildings that stood at the rear of the lots. Some people called them "privies", others "toilets", still others "outhouses". But to the kids they were always "shithouses", and it was their bounded duty, as kids, to see that not one shithouse was left standing anywhere in town on Hallowe'en night.

Every house had one. They ranged in rows along either side of the back lanes, all the same shape, and varying only slightly as to size and colour. Some were built into the corner of the fence so as to be harder to topple; some were anchored with wire attached to long iron stakes; some even had cement foundations. But over they all went, one after the other, right on their faces with a deep satisfying crunch.

Most people accepted the Hallowe'en raids as an upsetting fact of life, but not serious. They got up on the frosty November First morning, heaved the structure back into place, made the appropriate remarks about the younger generation, and let it go at that. The little house might need a few minor repairs, but still, things a lot worse than that could happen on Hallowe'en.

A few, however, never gave up the fight. Each year they planned and contrived how to beat the kids, and each year they lost. Larger stakes were driven into the ground, barbed wire was strung about, complicated warning devices laid out. Some even stood shivering in the shadows until midnight or beyond, waiting for kids who never came. Then no sooner were they back in the house than they'd hear the familiar creaking thump that told them the kids had outsmarted them again.

To a very few, the feud with the kids became an obsession, and the most seriously afflicted of these was old Bones McGuire.

Old Bones was the nearest equivalent to a junk dealer that the town had. Nobody knew where he came from or why he'd come to this new town all alone, but he'd had enough money to build himself a neat little shack on the outskirts, behind which he kept an enormous garden. He did odd jobs in the town, and took home any metal junk that nobody wanted. He collected his junk in an old two-wheel cart, pulled by a horse that looked as ancient as himself.

Much of his time he spent in the nuisance grounds, where he stuffed old bottles and bits of metal into a gunny sack and carted them home. Old Bones was even known to pay a few cents for disused articles, like metal buggy rims that would make good hoops, or old baby carriage wheels that could be converted into cars, bent hoes and rakes and rusty old horseshoes; such objects as are useless to grown-ups, but for which kids always have great need.

Perhaps this was the basis for the hatred that grew between Old Bones and the kids of the town. Or perhaps it was rooted in nothing more significant than that he lived alone and communicated with no one. Whatever the reason, the hatred grew, and Old Bones became the prime target for the Hallowe'en gangs. His toilet was a small, neat affair that stood anchored firmly by the high, whitewashed board fence that surrounded his back yard. So securely was it anchored that I'm sure that in the stark light of day the combined efforts of every kid in town couldn't have budged it. But on Hallowe'en night, when the devil lent muscles to their arms, half-a-dozen could have carried it out to the nuisance grounds.

In fact one night they did. The warped mind of Old Bones had produced fiendish schemes to beat the kids. One Hallowe'en, for instance, he went to the great trouble (working at night so none would know) of moving both outhouse and fence two feet forward. Since his was the pit type of convenience, this left a foul-smelling hole right where the kids would stand to push. This he covered with gunny sacks sprinkled with ashes to resemble the surface of the back lane. It worked. The first kids to dash up behind his structure fell headlong into the pit, and weren't fit company for anyone for the rest of the night.

The kids did nothing in retaliation except plan for the next Hallowe'en. Old Bones knew the same trick would never work again and frantically racked his brain for another. Finally, in desperation, he made a very ridiculous mistake. He determined to ambush the kids, catch the little buggers in the act. Then he'd show them. Where to hide? Not in the shadow of the house, that was too far from the privy. The corner of the fence wouldn't do, either. Inside the privy itself? Of course. The kids would never think of that.

To make sure that he wouldn't be taken unawares, he rigged up an elaborate system of signals consisting of binder-twine stretched ankle-high across the lane, tied to pegs and attached to a knocker that would bang on the side of the building. No kid could get past without warning the lurking Bones.

But, as happens to so many well-laid plans, everything went wrong. Compelled by some special instinct nature provides for Hallowe'en, the kids didn't come along the back lane at all. Came in through Old Bones front gate, in fact, and banged politely on his door to ask for apples. When there was no answer, they slid like shadows along the cinder path past his house and down to the privy. Soundlessly they went, pushed the wooden latch on the door that locked it from the outside, threw a rope around the top of the structure and pulled it forward on its face.

Then the bunch of them picked up the house with Old Bones inside and carried it across to the nuisance grounds where they left it. Nobody stuck around to see how Old Bones got out of the privy, but there was only one exit route – and, revolting as it was, the old man must have used it.

It was the next Hallowe'en after this incident that I first went out with the big kids. I was six, and going to school, so it was my due. My older brothers showed a singular lack of enthusiasm about taking me. "If you get caught it's your own fault," one warned.

"And don't tell anybody any names," the other added.

I don't know why Mother and Dad let me go out that night. Perhaps they were going to a Hallowe'en party themselves, and didn't pay much attention to what I was doing. At any rate, I remember my feeling when, dressed in a long coat and mittens with a toque pulled low over my ears, I ventured out in that frightful night.

It was pitch-dark, to begin with. No moon, clouds covering all the stars. The only light was the thin, yellow glow of coal-oil lamps that seeped through closely-drawn blinds. A raw north-west wind drove small white flakes of snow, and picked up old pieces of paper, whisking them about like ghosts in the dark. Far away across town came the occasional thump of a privy going over, the angry yapping of a dog, and running feet mixed with muted laughter. I waddled along on my short legs, never quite able to keep up with the gang, which continually grew in size until it numbered about twenty kids. Nor was I able to catch the whispered instructions that came from the gang leaders, so I tagged along, afraid of what was going to happen, but more afraid to go home by myself.

One of the kids in particular fascinated me. He carried a twenty-foot length of clothes-line rope which he'd made into a lasso. With this he practised endlessly, twirling it, throwing it over the shoulders of fleeing kids, even roping horses. He carried it everywhere, and had gained the name of "Rope" Parsons.

Down the dark back lanes we went. Past Bill Rath's barn. Rath was the drayman, and as this was nearing the time when he'd switch from wheels to runners, he'd left a waggon sitting behind the barn. Somebody picked up the tongue while the rest pushed and the waggon went down the lane with the gang. There was a hurried consultation about what to do with it. Somebody whispered, "Let's take it apart and put it up in the school!" But this had been done before, and besides it was too much work. So they shoved it into Mrs. Henry's garden and left it there.

Further along, an outhouse was pushed over, a gate taken from its hinges and hung high up on a telephone pole, a garden plough lifted from beside a barn and carried up on the Presbyterian minister's veranda. All warm-up stuff, really. Everybody knew who the real quarry was and very slowly, like migrating caribou, all the activities of the gang took us closer and closer to the backhouse of Bones McGuire.

As for me, I was tiring rapidly. My legs had never carried me so far so fast, and each time the gang spurted off after a prank I fell further behind. I didn't go home, though, partly because by now I wasn't sure of finding my way in the dark, and partly because of a compulsion to see the finish.

Finally, about midnight, the gang reached the lane behind McGuire's house. All talking stopped now; each member felt a hole in his stomach and a shakiness of the knees. Alone, none would have been capable of facing up to the task ahead; as a gang they moved with a compulsion beyond each member's volition.

Just as the first members of the gang came within fifty feet of the outhouse, a light appeared on top of it, shining down on the dirty faces in the lane. And a hollow voice, quivering with hatred, commanded, "You kids stop right there! I been waiting for you, see!"

Dead silence. Nobody moved. The faces stared as the pale glare of the flashlight glinted off the unmistakable shape of his shotgun.

"Go on, now, beat it," the voice from behind the light commanded, "or I'll use this gun on you." He probably intended to send a shot far over our heads, as others had been known to do, to scare the pants off us, but with Bones nobody was sure.

All the high-jinks and good humour poured out of the situation like clear water from a pail, to be replaced by the slops of hate. The old man stared down and the young stared back. Something very bad was happening. A voice of reason was needed. Somebody to laugh and say, "Okay, I guess the old boy got the best of us this time!" Billy Wilson almost did it, but he didn't have time.

Rope Parsons had faded back to the edge of the crowd, out of range of the light, had sneaked along the lane, climbed the board fence and dropped noiselessly into McGuire's garden. Nobody on either side twigged to what he was doing. And just as Billy Wilson stepped forward to say something that might have saved the situation, the clothesline rope snaked out, settled over Old Bones' shoulders, and jerked tight. Involuntarily the old man's fingers closed on the trigger. The full blast of two twelve-gauge shells roared into the night, and Billy Wilson fell forward on his face.

Nobody ran another step. Nobody moved. We just stood and stared. We could hear the old man's voice in the dark.

"What happened? I didn't mean to shoot. Oh God, nobody hurt, are they?"

"Billy's on the ground," somebody croaked into the night. "He ain't moving."

The old man slid off the outhouse and shone his flashlight down on the still figure. He began to sob and wail. "You kids saw it. I was caught from behind with that blasted rope. You saw it – didn't you?"

Nobody spoke.

"Oh Lordy," the old man wailed. "What did I go and do a thing like that for? Help me turn him over, will you?"

Nobody moved.

I edged my way forward until I could see Billy Wilson lying twisted on his face. Was that blood I saw beside him? Blood!

Old Bones had completely gone to pieces. "Ohhh, I'm done for," he wailed. "Done for now!" He gave the flashlight to a boy and tentatively put a hand out to touch Billy.

Then Billy was on his feet–laughing fit to kill–and all the other kids yelled and laughed, too. The lane was full of their laughter.

Everyone had a great time except Old Bones. He didn't laugh at all. The kids sure got the best of him that night.

6 *No Road Maps, No Road Signs, No Roads*

When I was seven years old we moved from the town of Nokomis to the city of Prince Albert. Before this move I had never been in a city. In fact, apart from my London-bridge-is-falling-down association with London, I hadn't even heard of a city. So we moved into a new world and in a sense into a new century – the world and century of running water, flush toilets and electricity. This is heady stuff for a seven-year-old, and the events of that move were forever etched in my memory.

Nineteen-nineteen was a pretty big year for us. That's the year Dad became mayor of Nokomis, beating out his arch rival Dr. Harding, and the year we got the Russell. The Russell was the first six-cylinder car in Nokomis. It may have been the first six-cylinder car in Saskatchewan for all I know, or in Canada for that matter. Perhaps in the world. At any rate that's the way we thought of her, because the Murphy's across the street owned only a model-T Ford, with a brass front and acetylene headlamps that had to be lighted with a match. Apart from a few other model-T's in town, I can't remember any other kinds of cars.

The Russell had many advanced features. A self-starter, for instance, by means of which you could turn the motor over with the push of a button instead of having to crank it–as you did with the Fords. There was a crank for it, of course, inserted through a hole just below the radiator, and used when the self-starter wouldn't work, which was often.

She was called a "touring car", and was in some ways like the modern convertible. That is, you could put the top up when it rained, but not by pressing a button. You had to get out and remove the cover from the top, which was folded up at the back, and then heave the whole thing forward and attach it to the windshield. There were no windows concealed in the doors to be rolled up when the weather was bad. You dug into the tool box and got out the side-curtains, which were also made of canvas with little isinglass windows in them. These domed onto the sides of the top. When everything was in place it was almost pitch-dark inside the car.

Every time we went out in the car it rained. And one would think that perhaps we might have developed some sort of drill for putting up the top and side curtains. Something like sailors have for battening down the hatches, or manning action stations, so that the whole operation could be executed with the maximum of speed and efficiency.

But we didn't. Instead, the action would develop something like this: we'd be driving along a dirt road over the prairie, on the way to Last Mountain Lake or Watrous, when Mother would say, "Listen, Warner, isn't that thunder?"

Dad would open his mouth to say something but before he got a chance a kid would say, "No, it's not going to rain. Just a couple of clouds."

Doris: "But if it does rain I'll get my hat all wet."

Hub: "That hat. I've seen better."

Phyllis: "I don't see why we should all suffocate just because somebody has a new hat."

This would go on until the rain began to pelt down. Then we'd all start to yell, Dad would stop the car, and we'd jump out and rush about getting the top up and the side-curtains in place, with Patsy yapping about and getting in everybody's way. By the time we got them buttoned on, and had climbed back into the dark dungeon of the car and started off down the road, with Dad trying to see out of the wet windshield (wipers hadn't been invented yet), a good half-hour would be gone. The car would splash along through the muddy ruts, throwing us about inside like hogs in a truck. Then we would get stuck.

There were three standard hazards to motoring in those days that have since disappeared. No, four. No, five. Besides having to put up tops and side-curtains, you also had to stop periodically and fill the radiator with water from a slough. In addition, there was always a good chance of getting stuck, getting lost, and having flat tires.

Take the matter of getting stuck. The roads of Saskatchewan were terrible. Nothing more than dirt trails, really. And the heavy soil of much of Saskatchewan is renowned for its moisture-holding qualities. It's called gumbo soil. It is extremely heavy and sticky, and it packs between the tire and fender of a car so tightly that the wheel can't turn. Then you have to get out, and with a sharp stick or a hoe or something, usually in the pouring rain, you dig the muck out.

Besides this, the roads were full of pot-holes. Low places, where the water would run and sit for days. Approaching one of these was always the same routine. Dad would stop the car and say, "Whups—what's this?"

Mother would say, "It looks deep, Warner."

One of the kids would say, "Heck, it's okay. Just give 'er the gun, Pop, and roar right through."

One of the girls would say, "We'll get stuck, I know we will."

Since there was no place to turn around, and no way of getting past the mud-hole, Dad would shift the Russell into low and proceed slowly into the middle of it, where we would sink quietly and serenely down to the axles. Then we'd fight over who was going to walk back to the nearest farm and get somebody to pull us out.

Finally somebody would walk back the mile–or two–or three–to the farm, and the farmer would hitch up his team and, whistling a merry tune, carrying the whiffle-trees in one hand and holding the reins in the other, he would come jangling down the road. He'd grin at us and say, "Still can't get along without the horse, eh?" and pull us out. The charge was always five dollars. There was some talk that farmers saw to it that the mud-holes near their farms never did completely dry up, but I'm not about to repeat that libel.

Getting lost was the next hazard. We were all right so long as we were driving only to Watrous Lake or to a sports day at Humboldt, say, but on longer trips we were hopeless. And for some reason, Dad decided that the best way to move the family from Nokomis to Prince Albert was to drive there in the Russell.

It beat travelling by Red River Cart, but that is exactly all you could say for it. There were no all-weather roads, gravelling was unknown. No highways of any kind, just roads a mile or so apart running each way. There were no signs on these roads, and no road maps to give direction. No motels dotted the sides of the road, and if you had to stay overnight you found a hotel in a town, or you went to a horrible thing called an "auto camp". Before we ever got near Prince Albert, we weren't at all sure that it mightn't have been easier, cheaper and probably more comfortable to have gone by Red River Cart.

We started out on a fine day near the end of June. All the household goods had been shipped in a railway car, which also contained Old Rosie, with enough feed and water to last her three days, a half-dozen bags of potatoes, and all of Mother's preserved peaches, pears, crab-apples, Saskatoon berries, and pickles. Doris wanted to ride in the car to protect her piano from falling over. We could only persuade her not to by pointing out that if it started to fall she couldn't stop it anyway.

With everything gone from it, the old cement-block house looked pretty bare, like a person from whom somehow all personality, emotion and concern has been removed. Mother stood for a long, long time at the front, just looking. She'd been happy here, happier and more prosperous than she would ever be again. Three of her children had been born in the big wooden bed behind that front bedroom window. She'd lived through the war here, and almost died during the influenza epidemic at the end of it. She was crying when she got into the car. Our mother cried easily.

So with the nine of us sticking out of that touring car in all directions, and Patsy complaining about his position on the floor, we started out. We got as far as MacDougal's garage and stopped. "I'll just have him check the oil before we start," Dad said. "Won't take but a minute."

Three hours later we were still there. At least the car was. Floyd MacDougal had found one or two other little things wrong. Like a hole in the radiator hose, and a blister on one of the tires as big as a baseball, and a maladjustment of the manifold. "She'll be fit as a fiddle in a minute or two," he told Dad happily. "You can stay here in the garage or do whatever you want."

Although Mother did her best to prevent it, Hub and I left the garage, took up with some evil companions who were going gopher snaring, and got our Sunday suits all wet and muddy. Patsy refused to leave the car and just sat on the back seat and barked, and that sound, along with Floyd

MacDougal banging away with his hammer was enough, as Mother said, "to drive a body mad".

I won't pretend that I can remember the details of the trip, but some episodes were so bizarre as to become part of Braithwaite folklore, and are told even to this day at one of our "family reunions" – which means any occasion when any group of the brothers and sisters numbering three or more are together, and have got into the sauce. Since family yarns of this nature tend to become amplified over the years, I can't swear to the exact and complete truth of the episodes – as I can to the rest of this book – but they are nevertheless worth repeating.

In the first place, after the old Russell finally dragged itself and us out of the garage and onto the hot, dusty road, I was hungry. Even at this early age my eating feats were memorable, it being pretty authentically recorded that on one Easter morning I single-handedly ate a dozen hard-boiled eggs, and one Shrove Tuesday, when the Wesley Church had a pancake supper for fifty cents a head, and all the young fry vied with each other, I ate forty-three-and-a-half pancakes. The good ladies of the Ladies' Aid, who were in charge of the caper, were laying bets on the side as to how long it would be before I had to go to the washroom and throw up. Nobody won.

The only other contest I ever won as a child also had to do with eating. At the Sunday School picnics they used to have races for all the boys and girls of different ages. And the prizes were wonderful – dollar watches, and jackknives, and water-pistols, and things like that. Once they even gave away a kite for first place, and oh Lord! how I wanted that kite. I wanted any of the prizes, in fact, and entered every race. I ran my chubby little heart out, but never managed better than fourth.

Then, at one picnic, some superintendent–perhaps inspired by my continued vain attempts to run faster than anybody–decided to have an eating race. The idea was to eat a dry soda biscuit and then whistle, eat another and whistle again, until six crackers had been consumed. This is much harder to do than to say.

But just as the other kids had the advantage over me in longer limbs and trimmer physiques, I had the advantage over them in eating. I was, you might say, in constant training. Naturally I won the race hands down, and joyfully looked forward to my prize. Now, by gawd, it was my turn. The Sunday School teacher approached me with a wide smile on his face, and one hand held behind his back. Then he made a little speech about my prowess as an eater, and even got a few laughs from the others. I didn't care, just so long as he produced that watch or knife or flashlight, or maybe even kite. Then, with a flourish, he brought his hand from behind his back and in it was–the remains of the box of crackers!

Where was I? Oh yes, in the Russell and hungry. Mother had put together an enormous lunch, big enough, as she said, "to feed a threshing gang". It consisted of several loaves of sandwiches, a dozen or so of her famous homemade buns, pounds of cookies, and a couple of cakes. Well, it might have fed a threshing gang, but it didn't go far with our bunch. I don't know what it is with kids in a car, but if there's food there, and they know it, they suffer the tortures of the damned until it's all consumed. Mother's lunch lasted us to Lanigan, a town about twenty-three miles due north of Nokomis. Then we were all hungry again.

Dad ignored our anguished cries and sped right through Lanigan and on to Humboldt. He knew both of these towns well, since his legal business had taken him there more than once, and the roads were familiar. But north of Humboldt we went out into unknown country with many turns in the road. And each time Dad turned a corner Mother would say quietly, "Why did you turn there, Warner?"

Dad never knew exactly why he had turned there, of course, and so he wouldn't say anything. But the rest of us would. We would begin a full-scale debate on which way we should have turned. Soon it would develop into a shouting match, whereupon my oldest brother, Morley, would threaten to "reach out", and the back seat would subside somewhat.

To make matters worse we were leaving the mixed grass region and entering into the aspen grove region. Or, to say it more simply, we were leaving the bald-headed prairie, where there were practically no trees, and entering the semi-bush country, where small groves of aspens break up the monotony of grass. This makes for good farm country, but it's harder for touring. The roads can no longer go straight, but are forced to occasionally wind around groves of trees and sloughs. It's easier to get lost.

Whenever we found ourselves completely lost, Dad would turn into a farmyard to ask directions, and we'd all pile out of the car to get a drink of water at the pump and stretch our legs. There was always a farm collie for Patsy to get into a barking match with, and in the midst of this racket, and with his kids shouting and running about all round him, Dad would try to get directions from a farmer who couldn't speak English.

Much of this area of Saskatchewan was settled by Ukrainians, Poles, Swedes, and other Europeans who had just recently come to Canada, and still couldn't speak the language. So Dad would stand there while the farmer, gesticulating wildly, would try to explain, "Go dees way . . . and dat way . . . den dees way again. . . ." Finally Dad would give up and get us all back into the car.

"I think I've got it now, Mother," he'd say, backing the car through a flock of fleeing hens and, accompanied by the yapping collie, we would go bumping down the rutted driveway. Within ten miles we'd be lost again.

Then we had the storm. Midsummer is tornado time, and the one we had on the twenty-seventh of June was a lulu. It was a hot day, and we'd put the top up to shade us from the sun. But that made it worse. Every time we stopped, the hot sultry air pressed down on the top of the car, and with no breeze at all to relieve it the nine Braithwaites were like birds in an oven.

Suddenly Phyllis yelled, "Look at that cloud. It's coming right at us!" And sure enough, rolling down the road in front was an enormous thunderhead. Then Hub yelled, "There's another one coming up behind!"

"Don't be silly," Doris told him "Clouds can't travel in opposite directions." But these two were. Tearing towards each other at a terrific speed. Then we heard the roar–like a hundred freight trains passing each other at full steam. The earth shook with it. Lightning split the clouds open, and a roar of thunder was added to the wind's roar.

Dad pulled quickly to the side of the road and stopped the car. "Hang on, everybody, it's a tornado for sure. There's not even time to put up the side-curtains." He'd no sooner said it than the lightning and thunder came again, and the roar was deafening. We happened to be right beside a farm, and to the left we could see the soil from the summer fallow twisting into air as though drawn up by a huge vacuum cleaner. Then, added to the roar of the thunder and wind and the sudden pelting rain on the canvas top, came the sickening sound of tearing timber. Before our eyes, the whole top of the big red barn took to the air.

Nobody in our car cried out. We just sat there and

stared. The great funnel of dust and debris passed on, the roar was gone. Then suddenly somebody shouted, "My God . . . they're naked!" and pointed towards the farmyard. And there, running around in helpless confusion, were half a dozen hens, each with scarcely a feather left on its body. The wind had plucked them as clean as any farm-wife ever could.

That was the storm. It cut a swath about ten yards wide across the field and through the farmyard. It did no damage whatsoever to the farm-house or granary or sheds or chicken-coop. Just the barn was in its path, and only the roof went with it. And where it went, nobody could see, for there was no trace of it anywhere. If that tornado had cut its swath a hundred yards to the left of where it actually passed, the old Russell and all its contents might well have disappeared as completely.

Only one more incident in that trip is worthy of report, and that was the crossing of the South Saskatchewan River, near St. Louis. None of us children had ever seen a river in our lives and, although Dad had described the Ontario Thames to us, where he used to fish as a boy, we had no real idea what a big river was like. And Dad had explained to us about the ferry that would carry us across the river.

"It's something like a big boat that we can drive the car right onto," he said.

"What makes it go across the river?" somebody asked.

"The current pushes on one side and a strong cable keeps the ferry from going downstream, so that it is carried across."

The only currants I was acquainted with were the red-currant bushes that grew near the fence back in Nokomis, and I can remember sitting there in the car pondering how they could ever carry a boat across a river. I had trouble with words like that. Once I was walking down the street with Dad in Nokomis, and he was talking to another man and he said, "Well, we'll have to register him right away." The word "register" caught my ear, and as I hurried along hanging onto Dad's big hand I worried over this. To me, "register" meant the hot air register at home, and I had a horrible mental picture of the two of them stuffing this other poor unfortunate down a register.

As we drew closer to the river there was less open prairie and more bush, and then we were there. Nothing anybody could have told us would have prepared us for that sight. There she was, the great South Saskatchewan, away below us at the bottom of a long, steep bank, winding like a great grey snake. And there, tugging at its cable on the shore, was the ferry, looking very small and fragile.

The road down to it was terribly narrow, terribly steep, terribly winding and terribly rough. In places it had been bolstered up with logs. Dad put the Russell into low and down we crept, growling like a complaining hippo. For once the Braithwaite family was silent. Slowly the Russell bumped and swayed and jerked its way to the water's edge and out onto the shaky ramp that led onto the ferry. At the other end of the ferry a logging chain was stretched from one side to the other, to prevent automobiles, we hoped, from running into the fast-flowing, muddy stream.

The ferryman, who was brown and tattooed and wore a tattered yachting cap, turned a big wheel at the side of the ferry, steering it into the current, and with a creaking of pulleys the rickety craft began to move out into the stream. Then the river was all around us. We were afloat. Nothing under us but water. The bank of the river we'd left was getting farther away and the bank on the other side was still far distant. At that moment I felt sure that what I wanted to do with my life was run away to sea.

Finally the ferry pulled into the other shore, the chain was lowered, the family loaded, and the Russell bumped its way ashore. And now it was put to its sternest test yet –

the challenge of climbing the steep, rough, winding road up the river bank.

Climbing hills was considered in those days to be the ultimate test of an automobile. A livery man at Watrous Lake, by the name of Telfer, had gained considerable fame because his Oldsmobile was reputed to be able to climb the steep bank from the lake up to the flat prairie in high gear. Nobody had actually seen him do it except the old man who cleaned up the public bathhouses. I remember as a five-year-old standing with some other kids while the old man gazed up the long hill, took his pipe from between his gums, and said with awe, "Yes, sir, Telfer can climb that 'ill in 'igh!"

But the Russell couldn't climb the river bank in high. Or in intermediate. Or in low. It simply couldn't climb it at all. It puffed and wheezed and groaned and literally blew its top. The radiator cap blew off and a jet of steam shot eight feet into the air. And then we had to go down to the river, fill a bottle with muddy water, and take it back to fill the radiator. After which we all got out and pushed, and the Russell strove mightily again, but there was no way it could get up that hill under its own power. We were stuck now for good. Doris said that we'd never get away from that dreary place, and that in years to come they'd find our skeletons, and tell all over the prairies how an entire family had perished on the river bank.

Hub and I and Phyllis didn't take it quite so badly. We located a great patch of Saskatoon berries and, although they weren't yet fully ripe, stuffed ourselves with them. Then we went down to the shore and got our feet wet in the river and Hub, trying to step on a log, fell right in.

Finally the ferry came back. This time its sole cargo was a farmer pulling a load of poplar poles with a team of oxen. Big brindle brutes, they were, the first we'd ever seen. Dad approached the man about pulling the Russell up the hill, but he wasn't interested. But Morley, who had been standing nearby, stated to Dad in a loud voice that he bet those stupid oxen couldn't pull the car anyway. That did it. The team was unhitched from the poplar poles and attached to the front end of the Russell. Then, with the car in low gear and the oxen straining and the rest of us pushing, we finally got the car moving. It was a frightful indignity for the Russell, however, and I don't think the old girl ever really got over it. Being hauled out of mud-holes by horses was bad enough. But oxen, really!

The rest of the trip to Prince Albert, a distance of about twenty miles, was uneventful. We were in bush country now – poplar, birch, some tamarack, and patches of spruce. About eight-thirty in the evening we reached the beautiful little city of about 5,000 people, perched on the north bank of the North Saskatchewan River, and a new life began for us all.

7 *Prince Albert – I Love You*

Many of the people who study such matters hold the view that the impressions one receives between the ages of six and twelve are the most vivid and lasting of all. That the environment of those years becomes your spiritual home for life.

I believe it.

Those were the years I spent in Prince Albert, Saskatchewan, and Prince Albert country became a part of me. Trees – long shadows cast by pine and spruce. The dry, harsh sound of the cicadas in the hot woods. Crunchy ground beneath. Sloughs, where blackbirds linger and hell-divers disappear and come up again a hundred feet away. Croaking frogs, glass jars with strings of jelly eggs waiting to hatch. Bare feet in the nettles. Dogs, rabbits, timid little snakes, bullies. Pinching cold of the north wind. Swooshing down icy hills on bob-sleds, with the wind ringing in your ears and the snow closing your eyes. That's Prince Albert and boyhood.

The place began as a trading post on the North Saskatchewan River, where intrepid Scottish and English and Irish empire-builders traded gaudy trinkets for glossy beaver pelts. And loaded these into *voyageur* canoes to be carried down-river, through the rapids, into Lake Winnipeg and thence, by way of the Hayes or Nelson rivers, to York Factory where they were loaded on sailing vessels and taken to London, to make top hats for dandies.

Some of them made the longer canoe trip across Lake Winnipeg, through the Lake of the Woods-Rainy River route to the Great Lakes, and then down the Ottawa to Montreal. A canoe trip that took months.

It was those same intrepid Britishers who so generously sowed their seed in the Indian maidens to produce a new race of frontiersmen called the Métis. And it was the Métis, skilled rivermen, guides, Red River Cart drivers, buffalo hunters, who were the first permanent settlers in the Prince Albert area. Many of their descendants were among Prince Albert's most prominent citizens.

Following the usual pattern, the traders were followed by the missionaries. In this case, James Nisbit from Scotland, who had been a Sunday School teacher at age thirteen and a Sunday School superintendent at age sixteen. In 1866 he, with his wife and child and some friends, trekked across the plains from Winnipeg. It took them forty days to make the trip, and there were no motels or hotels, or even towns, in which to spend the night. That was even tougher travelling than we did in the old Russell.

Dad moved his family to Prince Albert full of high hopes. He had a partnership with an old Ontario school chum, S. J. Branion, the leading lawyer in the city, which was also the judicial centre for a very wide area. As befits a leading citizen, he bought–and took a mortgage on–the second largest house in town, which stood at the top of the Second Avenue hill at the corner of 21st Street. And when our bunch hit that house we nearly wrecked it there and then.

I've moved into many different houses in my time, but the memory that sticks in my mind most vividly is that of our first night in the Prince Albert house. A number of circumstances accounted for our actions, I guess. First of all, we'd never seen a house like it. The Nokomis house had no running water, no electricity, no flush toilet, no porcelain bathtub, no hot-water radiators. The house in Prince Albert had all these things.

Secondly, the seven of us had just been released from a twelve-hour trip that, to say the least, had been eventful. We were like a herd of colts when first let out of the barn in the spring. Light-hearted, giddy, and reckless.

Thirdly, we were – and I have to admit this – a crazy bunch. There is, I'm afraid, no other way to describe us. We were wild, undisciplined, inquisitive, and audacious. I don't know what made us that way. Perhaps it was the prairie wind beating constantly against our eardrums. Perhaps it was the prairie cold, or the prairie flatness, or the prairie mosquitoes that punctured our hides, or just the downwright craziness of the prairies themselves. Anyway, we were a crazy bunch.

Maybe it was the look of the house itself, sitting there on the corner, surrounded on two sides by a low concrete wall. On this, at intervals of about thirty feet, were mounted solid round concrete balls, each about the size of a basketball, each on a square, ornamental pedestal. They looked like a row of bare-faced busts and then, after one of us had painted faces on them, like a row of cartoon busts. The house had a big round tower thing in its front corner, surmounted by a sort of steeple.

When Dad turned the key in the front door and opened it, we rushed past him like a destroying wind. We found the front hall electric light switch and turned it on. "Hey, look!" we shouted. "Lights!" Then we switched them off and on a dozen times and proceeded to the other rooms to repeat the magic there.

Hub and I had to go wee wee, and when advised by Mother that we were to go upstairs instead of in the back yard we took the stairs two at a time to see if such a thing could be true. Sure enough it was. And then when we flushed the toilet and everything was flushed out we proceeded to investigate how big a load could be disposed of. For anyone who's interested, the toilets of that day would handle half of the Prince Albert *Herald*. A whole newspaper plugged it and flooded the bathroom floor.

We also discovered that when you rolled marbles down the bathtub, and they swirled around on the porcelain before going down the drain, they made a marvellous sound. We had to abandon that game, however, due to a shortage of marbles.

There was a radiator in the hall, and when you tapped it with a hammer it gave off a different note for each section. I was doing this and making pretty good music, I thought, going from one end to the other. Unfortunately, I also hit the little metal tap at the end of the radiator and broke it off. Water shot out against the wall and I stuck my finger over it and yelled for Dad. It took him quite a while to whittle a little stick the right size to plug it. That stick plug stayed in the radiator all the time we lived in the Prince Albert house.

But the culmination of our adventures came at about nine-thirty, when Dad had just learned, by frantically phoning the freight sheds, and then the home of the station agent, that the reason our furniture hadn't arrived yet was because the car carrying it had been side-tracked at Wakaw, and wouldn't be along for a couple of days.

"Oh pshaw, what about Rosie?" he said. "She'll starve." (Actually Rosie survived the ordeal by chewing the upholstery off the parlour chairs. A remarkable cow.)

"We'll just have to make the best of it," Mother said. "I'll borrow some cots and bed-sheets from the neighbours. Come on, Morley," she added. "We'll go calling."

It was then that the lights went out. Every light in the house. A boy who had grown tired of turning lights on and off, was doing a further investigation of the intricacies of the electrical system. In those days, houses didn't have wall-plugs as they do now – at least this house didn't. Instead, there were wall-sockets into which a bulb or a plug could be screwed. On peering into one of these, he noticed a little screw. Now a screw calls for a screwdriver and he soon found one. But as soon as the metal of the screwdriver touched the live wire he got a terrific shock, yelled, and dropped the tool. At the same time, every single light in the house went. There was dead silence for a few seconds, then loud, anguished cries from the girls who were upstairs staking claims on their bedrooms. Nobody could see a thing, and in the strange house everybody was lost. It took Dad at least twenty-seven minutes to find the fuse, which was located deep in the cellar behind the furnace. I don't know why, but in those days all fuse boxes were located behind the furnaces.

We finally got settled into the big house and went about the various businesses of our lives: Dad, to try to make a living for a family of nine in the face of a shattering drop in legal work, which was caused by the formation of a new judicial district to the north; Mother, to the task of keeping a big family clothed and fed and warm on less and less money; and the rest of us to just being kids.

One of our projects that year was to establish a dog team. The winters were long and cold in Prince Albert, and during the winter months there was still considerable trapping going on in the forests to the north. And occasionally, down on River Street where the fur-buyers' shops were, we'd see a trapper come in with a team of dogs. This was too much; we had to have a dog team of our own.

To make the matter more urgent, we already knew a couple of kids who had dogs that pulled them on sleds. One boy, by the name of Jim Marvin, had lost a leg in some sort of accident before we knew him. He wore an artificial leg, but it was a clumsy thing, and we always liked to go swimming with him in the big slough because then he would remove the leg with his clothing and go hopping down the shore and into the water. We never tired of watching him do this.

Well, Jim had a little brown collie-type dog named Rusty, who was the greatest sled-puller I've ever known. Each morning in the winter Jim would hitch him to the sled, and down the snow-covered road Rusty would tear, barking gleefully. Then he would hang around the school, passing the time of day with the other dogs, until Jim needed to be pulled back home again.

So we had to have a dog team of our own. For a while we considered Patsy as a possible lead dog, but we couldn't find a harness small enough for him; besides, he'd bite us every time we started to put any harness on him, and then would lie down and refuse to budge. So we began collecting stray dogs. There were a lot of them around, skinny, mangey, pitiful curs of all sizes who for some reason had left home and become wanderers.

We would entice these lean and hungry canines into the barn at the back of the lot where Old Rosie was kept, and lock them in the stall with her. Then we'd go to the butcher and beg some bones and meat scraps with which to feed them. "Once you feed a dog," Hub explained, "he'll stay with you forever." But we never tested this theory by letting them out of the barn.

Finally, we had gathered together six of the weirdest-looking dogs imaginable. To say they were of mixed parentage would be a gross understatement. We gave them names gleaned from a reading of Jack London and other writers of stories about heroic dogs, on the theory that if they had good names they'd try to be good dogs.

There was Buck, for instance, who Hub maintained

"had St. Bernard in him". He may have at that, but he also had some hound, some Pekinese, maybe a little bulldog and a million fleas. All he ever wanted to do was sit and scratch those fleas. There were Rex and King, Prince and White Fang and Kazan. There was even one we wanted to call "Barree, son of Kazan", but it turned out to be somebody's daughter. So we called her Queenie.

Somehow we managed to get harness for them all. Some of it was made of rope, some of rags, and some of it even had a bit of leather in it. One set that was fitted out for White Fang, a small, all-black cocker-spaniel (*basically*, he was cocker-spaniel) with the saddest eyes I've ever seen, was made of rags from somebody's bright green dress. When we tied it on White Fang his big, sad brown eyes spoke of all the meanness and misery in the world.

Finally, we hitched the dogs to a sled, and then both Hub and I sat on it. The dogs also sat down in the snow and went about the business of scratching fleas, smelling each others' rear ends, or licking their private parts. They had no intention of repaying our hand-outs of meat and bread-scraps with a little work. Where had we got that idea?

So we stood up and threatened and threw frozen horse turds at them, and cajoled and tried to behave like dog-team drivers. "Mush, King! Mush, Queenie! Come on, Prince!" It sounded as though we had captured a royal family. But nothing worked. I honestly believe not one of those dogs had ever heard the word "mush" before.

Suddenly a miracle happened in the form of an old rattle-trap truck that came wheezing down Second Avenue. Practically nobody drove his car in the winter time then, preferring to put it up on blocks in a garage. If you did drive, you had to drain the water from the radiator every time the car was stopped for more than half an hour. But this individual was one of the daring pioneers of automobile travel. He'd fitted the wheels with chains so that they could grip the snowy road, he'd strapped an old buffalo robe over the hood, and he'd slid a piece of cardboard over the radiator. The result was pretty fearful-looking, and pretty noisy, too.

And it just so happened that at that moment Buck decided to live up to his name as a strong, fearless, relentless pursuer. Maybe he'd had experience with cars before. Maybe he mistook the buffalo robe for his girl-friend. At any rate he issued a deep "Woof!" and took off after the rattling truck.

It wouldn't have been so bad if he'd been the lead dog. But situated as he was – fourth in the team – his sudden acceleration tended to disrupt the order. In fact, it scattered them all over the place, and for a minute all we could see was legs and ears and bits of calico harness, accompanied by much yelping and barking. Then the whole team became operational, but unfortunately not according to the original plan. The dogs were hitched to pull in tandem rather than abreast. And they definitely weren't supposed to race each other.

But race they did, determinedly and vociferously. As the slower dogs lagged behind, the others dragged them along until the harness ripped apart. The whole outfit disappeared into a large bush across the road. We never did see any of those dogs again. Here and there we found bits of harness clinging to a twig or bramble. But no sign at all did we ever find of dogs. They had absolutely no sense of gratitude. Hub summed it up by saying, "Once a bum, always a bum!"

But if we never did manage to get dogs to pull us, we did have a lot of fun coasting down the long Second Avenue hill and other hills in the town. One of these was called "Devil's Dip", and as a place to commit suicide it had few equals.

Prince Albert is built on the river bank, so that half the

city is on the flat land above and half of it on the flat land down on the river level. Most of the avenues, Central Avenue, First and Second etc., are hills. Some of them long and gradual, others short and steep. As the winter wore on, their roads and sidewalks became hard-packed with snow which gradually turned to ice. The streets became one giant bob-sled run.

To take advantage of this situation, Hub invented a special bob-sled. It was none of your low, wide, sluggish contraptions, as sold by Eaton's catalogue. No, this one was long and slim and speedy. To make it, Hub simply took a 2-by-8-inch plank about eight feet long. To one end he attached a narrow sled with steel runners, worn smooth. At the front he placed another sled, but this one was on a swivel so that it could be turned by means of a stick nailed across the front runners. Two-by-fours between sled and plank held it about a foot off the ground. This home-made bob-sled would accommodate half a dozen kids, and would go like the wind.

Hub appointed me as steerer, and he was pusher. That meant that I lay down at the front on my belly with my hands on the steering-stick. The other kids sat close together, each holding the feet of the one behind. At the end was Hub, who would run about fifty yards, pushing for all he was worth and then kneel on the back as the bob-sled sped on its way.

The Second Avenue hill was fully three blocks long, and I'm sure we gained speeds of over sixty miles an hour, and the momentum would carry us for another couple of blocks. It was a good slide.

There was, however, one small problem. At the bottom of the last block, just where the bob-sled would be travelling at maximum speed, there was a railway track. In fact, the main railway track. When our steel runners crossed the steel rails of the crossing sparks flew and we slowed down just a little. But worse than that, there was always the remote chance that a train and the bob-sled would reach that point on the rails at exactly the same instant.

The Braithwaite bob-sled became famous on Second Avenue hill. We could beat anything that showed up. Races were always in the dark, of course, because it was dark by the time school was out, and besides during the day time there were too many loads of coal or wood or groceries being hauled up the hill by struggling teams of horses with sharp cleats on their shoes. So, under the faint, eerie glow of street lamps, we whizzed down the hill, shouting and laughing and trying to cut the other bob-sled off and spill its riders in the snow.

Across the road from our house was a boys' college run by the Anglican Church. It was a big brick building with a huge yard. What I remember best about it was that they had a big outdoor rink, and sometimes they would let us skate on it. But mostly we fought with these kids–them being Anglicans and us being Methodists–or engaged in some sort of competition with them.

One winter, having observed how much fun we were having on our bob-sled, they got busy and made one of their own. At first they were no match for us, but they gradually increased in speed and skill to the point where they issued a challenge. A race down Second Avenue from 20th Street, where the steepness really began, down to the bottom, to the first street past the tracks.

Hub was gleeful. "We'll show those juicers who's the fastest," he gloated. "They may have a rink and a tennis court, but we've got the best sled."

The night chosen for the race was clear and cold. There was no wind and the snow was so crisp it crackled when you walked on it. The frosty air made circular haloes around the tiny street lamps. The sky was full of stars, and the northern lights swayed like great coloured ghosts overhead.

One of the teachers from the college came out to act as official starter and, since we had no adult of our own to represent us, we grudgingly accepted his services. We had six kids and they had six. Their team was a little heavier than ours, which gave them something of an advantage. But we had experience and slightly slicker runners on our sled.

We got on our bob-sleds at the top of the hill. Each kid had his toque pulled down as low over his forehead as he could get it, and his face hidden behind a woollen scarf. Then, at the signal from the starter, the two pushers began their run and the race was on. Hub was a good pusher, so we gained a slight lead. Lying at the front of our sled, keeping her as straight as possible for every advantage, I could hear the rattle of the other bob's steel runners on the icy snow slightly behind us. Our boys crouched low, each tucking his head against the back of the boy in front to cut down the wind resistance, and urged the sled forward with their bodies.

Faster and faster we went, the wind cutting like a knife. And then I heard it. A freight train on the tracks below. I could see the beam of the headlamp cutting through the frosty air. We were going to reach the crossing just about the same time as that train.

There was only one thing to do. Cramp the steering-sled hard to the right. For a horrible moment it slid sideways, then the steel runners caught and the bob-sled went over, with all of us tumbling on the road and sprawling along on the hard snow. We had just managed to sit up when we saw to our horror that the other bob wasn't stopping. It was heading straight towards that slow-moving freight, and there was no help for it. Maybe the steerer had panicked and couldn't move. As we sat there, petrified, the bob roared straight towards the centre of one of those freight cars. Then every one of those kids leaned back and flattened himself against the bob and underneath they went at the exact spot of maximum clearance half-way between the front and rear trucks of that car.

There wasn't a sound from anyone for a long time. We just sat and stared. When the freight finally passed, there they were, the six of them standing holding on to the rope of their bob-sled, waiting to come across. Not one had been touched.

Always after that I had a strong, strong suspicion that maybe there was some truth in the theory that the Anglicans were God's special people, and forever in His care.

The best thing about Prince Albert, however, was the Strand Theatre on Central Avenue. It was a temple of delight, an arena of excitement, a steam bath of emotions, a great place to be on Saturday afternoon. Movies on Saturday afternoon cost a nickel for kids, and on Friday night they cost a dime. So, of course, we always wanted to go on Friday night. But there weren't enough dimes to go around.

We'd line up at Dad's chair after lunch on Saturday and he would dig deep into his pocket with his big hand and produce a handful of change. Then, with a long finger, he'd poke among the dimes and quarters and coppers, looking for nickels. (I remember that there was always a shiny lucky quarter in that big, lean hand. Dad had carried it in his pocket since he was a school-teacher in Ontario.) Then he'd dole out the nickels, and we'd be off.

For a long time Denny got in free, so Hub and I would take him with us. Dad, who paid little attention to these niceties, didn't know about the free ticket and so he gave us a nickel for Denny, too. Which meant a whole raft of cent candy, licorice plugs, licorice whips, jaw-breakers and candy kisses to be munched during the performance.

We worked this racket until long after Denny was six. He was a skinny kid and small and the ticket-seller got used to letting him in free. But they changed ticket-sellers, and when we appeared the new one asked,

"How old is the little red-headed boy?"

"Oh, he's just five," Hub assured her.

But he hadn't reckoned on Denny's pride of accomplishment in having achieved his sixth birthday three months earlier. He elbowed his way to the front with fire shooting from his eyes and stated defiantly, "I'm not five. I'm six!" That was the end of our nickel's worth of goodies during the show.

Inside that dark theatre it was bedlam. Every kid that came considered it his duty to make as much noise and create as much mayhem as possible. We always arrived at least a half-hour before the show started, and for some silly reason they let us in (the practice of making kids line up outside on the sidewalk evidently hadn't been considered). So, we whiled away the time wrestling, stealing each other's toques and mitts, shoving each other under the seats, chasing each other up and down the aisles and yelling our heads off.

Then–at last–would come the long-awaited signal. The lights would go out, and the trademark of the Union Operator would flash on the screen. And the roar was such as greets a tie-breaking home run in the ninth with two out. And when the movie began there was still no need to be quiet. There was no talk or sound–except what came from the eager piano player in the pit–and all the dialogue was printed on the screen. So you could cheer with the good guy, scream at the bad guy, and laugh your head off at the funny guy without ever interrupting the action.

And what action! It was all action then. We'd see at least four items. A feature, usually starring William S. Hart, or Doug Fairbanks, or Hoot Gibson, or Milton Sills, or Thomas Meighen. They were the greatest: plenty of fist-fights, thousands of blank cartridges blazed away, breakneck chases, crashing aircraft, exploding ships. Talk about violence! They were loaded with violence.

And then came the serial. Continued from last week, when the heroine, always in riding breeches, had been bound hand and foot and locked inside a shack which was perched precariously on the edge of a cliff. The villain, bad cess to him, had planted a charge of dynamite – they used more dynamite in the movies than they did in construction in those days – and was lurking behind a boulder, ready to push the plunger down and blow shack and heroine to eternity.

But it never worked out that way. The hero, you see, was on the way. He always got there in the nick of time and saved her life. Then she would throw her arms around his neck, and kiss him, and flutter her eyelashes, and such a "boo!" went up from the disgusted boys in the audience as could be heard clear down River Street.

And then there was the comedy, which we all loved. One- and two-reelers, featuring Charlie Chaplin, or Fatty Arbuckle, or cross-eyed Chester Conklin, or wistful Harry Langdon, or deadpan Buster Keaton. There was always a chase with automobiles just missing each other on busy streets, with men piling out of them and flying through windows, and lots of prat-falls – the pie in the face came much later – and the Keystone Cops, and the Mack Sennett bathing beauties.

It was all pantomime, and it killed us. I have never heard such laughter as arose from those Saturday afternoon audiences. Never since have I laughed so hard that I couldn't get my breath, that my stomach pained, that I literally fell out into the aisle. Yes, I admit it, more than once our bladders couldn't stand the strain, and many a wet-legged kid staggered embarrassed out of the Strand. No generation of kids ever laughed as hard as we did, I'm sure, and none had so much to laugh at. It was truly the golden age of laughter.

The serious shows, too, could get to us if they were broad enough and mawkish enough to make us cry. *Over the Hill to the Poor House* is one that did the trick. There was this old couple, see, who gave everything to their children. The youngest child begged them not to, but they wouldn't listen to him, and the rest of the family practically threw him out of the house. But then the time came when the old couple were sick and weak, and there was nowhere for them to go but the poor-house. Finally, the youngest son arrived, too late to save them, but on their deathbeds they forgave him, and there wasn't a dry eye in the Strand.

But the greatest of all the shows we saw in Prince Albert – it must have been toward the end of our years there – was *Robin Hood*, starring Douglas Fairbanks.

There's never been another movie like it. There never can be. Denny and I wanted to go to that show so badly we could scarcely wait until Saturday afternoon. We begged and begged for a dime for Friday night, but Dad wouldn't or couldn't provide it. So, since we just couldn't wait around the house, we went out and played in the deep snow-drifts beside the jail field. We rolled down them and tunnelled into them and ran through them until we were so covered with snow as to be unrecognizable. And so tired we could hardly drag ourselves home. The next day was *Robin Hood*.

The show was everything we'd hoped for. Full of adventure, and humour, and pathos, and suspense. Those wonderful, wonderful scenes in Sherwood Forest, with the men in Lincoln green running up and down the slanting trunks of those great oak trees, and the sun slanting through the leaves. The scenes in the castle, when Robin Hood and his men finally attacked, and the sword fight. Ah those sword fights! Doug Fairbanks could jump ten feet in the air from a standing start, I'll swear he could. Those other guys just didn't have any chance against him at all. And the way he could shoot that arrow. Wow!

After the show, as we puffed our way up the long Second Avenue hill, our frozen breath shooting out like smoke, we went over those marvellous scenes in Sherwood Forest again and again. And from then on, Robin Hood became our game. We made bows from the oak ribs of binder canvases, and arrows from long sticks, with nails fastened to the ends, filed down to needle sharpness. And we shot at everything that moved.

If you remember – as I do – the great movies of the early 1920's, don't try sitting up to watch them again on the late, late show. They're not the same movies that made us die laughing, cheer our throats sore, and cry big tears. They can't be. Why, they often look kind of silly. I don't know what they've done to them, but they're certainly not the same movies. Don't watch them. They'll make you laugh and cry all over again, but not in the same way.

8 *Chums*

From London, England, to Prince Albert is a distance of approximately four thousand miles as the crow flies, and to get from London to Prince Albert in the early 1920's, by ship and train, would take at least twenty days. But in other respects, the two cities were close as brothers. In the matter of reading material for instance.

Much of what we read in Prince Albert came directly from London. *The Illustrated London News*, *Punch*, *The Spectator*, and other publications were in many homes; but so far as we were concerned, the piece of pure literary gold, the ultimate in fantasy, adventure and excitement was bound up in a big, red hard-covered publication called *Chums*.

The big, red book, at least eight by ten inches in size and two inches thick, contained a variety of good things to gladden any boy's heart. There was always a story about English public school life. This bore absolutely no relation to the public school we attended, and it fascinated us. There were "masters" for instance, and "fags" and "head boys". Also, the boys lived in the school, and played strange games called rugger and cricket, of which we had never heard. These stories were always peopled with the same kind of boys. A thin one, with glasses, and a fat one, with a sweet in his hand. We didn't know what a "sweet" was, but it looked like a piece of cake or a cookie. And there was always a misunderstood boy who was having a hard time getting on with the others, but Lord! how noble he was, and brave. He'd *never* snitch on another boy, no matter what bad thing the other might do, and he always took his canings like a man.

Then there was always a story about pirates. This also was something so far removed from Prince Albert as to be from another world entirely. Men who went to sea in wooden sailing ships, and fired round-shot at each other, and sliced each other up with cutlasses. Terribly fierce men they were. Talk about violence on modern television! I've never seen anything to equal those pictures in *Chums*. There would be a man standing at the end of a plank, and another prodding his posterior with a cutlass, and the water below full of sharks grinning hideously up at him. That was enough to give you nightmares for a week.

And there was always a serial about the American wild west, with rustlers and gun-fighters, and the lonesome man searching for his identity. And a story about the French Revolution based on the "Scarlet Pimpernel" idea. The one I remember best was *Jackolantern*, which was all about a mysterious rescuer of aristocrats who gave off a peculiar glow when he ran through the night.

Science, too, had its place. *Gold a Mystery* was a perfect example, and it featured a scientist who had discovered a method for turning lead into gold. Needless to say, there were a number of nefarious characters after his secret who wanted to use it to "rule the world". Then, as now, in popular fiction, some rotten type was always trying to get control of the world.

There were stories of people lost in the Arctic and others lost in the tropics, and being swallowed by giant, grinning snakes. Stories of India, stories aboard Chinese junks, stories of Africa. And always one white man was a match for those hordes of ferocious savages which surrounded him, and always "right" was synonymous with "white", and inevitably British fair play and justice triumphed in the end, after a satisfactory slaughter of vile aborigines.

All the stories were in serial form, which suggests that *Chums* was actually a boys' magazine, with the twelve issues or twenty-four or whatever, bound together to make an enduring book. Besides the stories, there was a great variety of puzzles, jokes, things to make, things to do, magic tricks. None of these appealed to me much, since I've never been much interested in guessing riddles, manipulating cards, or putting things together. But the fiction! I'm sure that the English writers of stories for boys must have reached the high point of their artistry during that era.

We got *Chums* for Christmas the year I was seven. Mother began to read the stories to Denny and Hub and me. She'd sit in front of the enormous fireplace, with the three of us scattered around on the rug, and read to us in her soft Irish voice. Each night, one instalment. And since that's where the story stopped, she stopped, too, and no amount of argument, cajolery, blandishments or threats could get her to go further.

Three things happened, inevitably, as a result of Mother reading *Chums* to us. One was that we got pretty mixed up about the English and the British Empire. The second was that I developed a great liking for exciting, suspenseful, violent, fast-moving, imaginative adventure stories. And thirdly, I learned to read much faster than I otherwise would have done.

I simply couldn't wait until the next reading session to find out what happened in the story, and so I'd get hold of *Chums* and read it myself. This did queer things to my vocabulary. Since I didn't know the meanings of some of the big words I encountered, and since I hadn't yet started using dictionaries, I just sort of guessed at the meanings. I also guessed at the pronunciations. I went around saying things like "intimate" for "intimidate".

The school we smaller members of the family attended in Prince Albert was named, naturally, King George. Dad took Phyllis and Hub and me to school, and introduced us to the principal, a tall, horse-faced man with two enormous front teeth, by the name of Maurice Werner, who had a mean eye and a powerful right hand. Try as I may, I can't think of one good thing to say for Maurice Werner, or for his school. One of the *worst* things I remember is that Werner had the strange notion that the ability to spell somehow entered the head through the hand. Thus, for having mistakes in spelling we were sent to the office, where Maurice pounded away at our hands with a long rubber strap. I can truthfully report that this method of teaching spelling doesn't work. When Hub and I went to King George School we were both poor spellers. When we left, our hands were tougher, our dispositions meaner, and our respect for the reasonableness of adults considerably reduced, but there was no noticeable improvement in our spelling.

When Dad led us into that big, ugly, two-storey brick building that spring, Hub was in Grade Three, and I was in Grade One. We went to our respective rooms–this school was big enough to have one grade to a room–trustingly placing our destiny in the hands of adults who we'd been taught were, by definition, worthy of respect.

The morning, except for a few routine questions and hostile stares, was uneventful. At recess we went out and faced the city kids, with whom we sparred warily like strange dogs meeting for the first time. After recess, things were going on well. I'd been handed a dog-eared primer and some plasticine, and was beginning to take notice of my strange surroundings when the back door of the room opened, and the Grade Two teacher poked her head in. After a whispered consultation with our frowning teacher, the two of them stood aside and Hub was ushered into the room.

He had a look on his face that he was never again to lose in school. Cold, semi-amused, defiant. He took a vacant seat at the back of the outside row, the biggest seat in the room but still too small for him. Head held high, he surveyed the inquisitive faces squirmed around to gawk at him and, much to their delight, favoured them with an exaggerated wink.

What had happened was so stupid that even now I find it hard to believe. During the course of some routine tests the Grade Three teacher discovered that Hub couldn't spell the words he should have been able to spell. So, determined not to be put upon, she marched to the principal and complained that this boy from Nokomis had obviously been shoved ahead without regard for his scholastic achievement, and should never have reached Grade Three.

"We can't have that," said Maurice Werner. "Put him back to Grade Two."

The Grade Two teacher, finding the same deficiency, put him back to Grade One. Hub's comment at noon was caustic. "If they'd put me back any further they'd have had to kick me out of school."

Naturally enough, this action of the teachers finished Hub's school career. It was patently obvious to him that he was dealing with nincompoops, so he treated them with the scorn they deserved. Of all the lickings he got from Maurice Werner for bad spelling, not one ever brought a tear to his eye. And, when the going became too rough, he simply played hookey. The year we left Prince Albert he played hookey for an entire month without our parents discovering the fact. He'd leave for school in the morning, come home for lunch, then apparently leave for school again afterwards.

By the time we left Prince Albert, Hub had managed to filter his mis-spelled way up to Grade Four. Encountering considerably more understanding for his affliction in Saskatoon, he managed to make it up to Grade Six. By then he was sixteen and could legally quit school, which he did with a great sigh of relief, to enter the real world where people are judged by what they can do rather than how well they can spell.

Possessing an abundance of natural skill, energy, practical common sense, and a willingness to work ten times as hard as his rivals, he naturally prospered. He ultimately became the head of a large dairying concern and a pillar of the community. So much for the teachers who promised him reform school, jail, and skid row.

There were a lot of English, Scots and Irish in Prince Albert in the early Twenties, a result of the pre-war wave of immigration that, in 1913, brought more than 400,000 newcomers to Canada. Many of them lived in a sort of ghetto on the south end of town known as the "English Settlement". They were mostly Londoners, a lot of them Cockneys, and they were a rugged, pugnacious group. They taught us how to play soccer, and then beat the pants off us at every match.

But the Britisher I remember best was Nigel Spencer, the boy who faced up to the bully. Nigel's father had been a sergeant in the British army in India. Straight as a ramrod he was, and full of those old-fashioned army virtues, such as bravery, resourcefulness, manliness, devotion to duty, and these he instilled into his son.

Nigel's house was full of exotic treasures from India, wicked, long, curved scimitars, turbans and hookas. He even had an eight-foot-long cobra skin. Perhaps it was this which gave Nigel his love of snakes, but in any case he always kept a number of these creatures as pets. They were red-sided garter snakes, the only kind found as far north as Prince Albert, and they were pretty, timid little things. He kept them in wire cages in a tent in which we also used to sometimes sleep. On occasion, they'd get out and crawl under our blankets for warmth. I think that's where I lost any fear of snakes that I might ever have had.

Not far from Nigel's house on Twenty-first Street there lived a bully named Art Forester. He was a real honest-to-gawd bully of the type we sometimes read about in *Chums*. And he hated snakes. So his particular target for bullying was Nigel Spencer, who was about eight inches shorter and at least twenty pounds lighter than he.

Art would wait for Nigel after school and push him in a ditch, or steal his cap and put it in the mail-box or punch him in the nose. Life became pretty hectic for Nigel who, although he was a fast runner, couldn't seem to keep out of Art's clutches. None of the rest of us would help our chum, of course, because we knew that if we did Art would start bullying us. That was understood and accepted.

Finally, although he knew it was not in the best tradition of English schoolboy honour, Nigel was reduced to telling his father about this.

Sergeant Spencer drew himself up to his full five-feet-eight-inches, threw out his chest and his handle-bar moustache bristled. "What's this? A bully? And you are snitching on him?"

"Well, he won't leave me alone. Yesterday he took half my dibs from me and shot them away in his catapult."

"And what did you do?"

"What could I do?"

"You could have stood up for yourself like a man and threshed him."

"Threshed him! Gosh, Dad, have you ever seen this guy? He's twice as big as I am."

"Makes no difference. He's a bully, and bullies are always cowards."

"They are?"

"Absolutely. That's why they're bullies. If you stand up to this fellow and let him know you won't stand for any more of his bullying, he'll. . . ."

"He'll kill me! That's all!"

"Better a dead hero than a live coward, my boy. But he won't kill you. The thing is to attack him suddenly, with all the vigour you can muster, do you see. Take the blighter by surprise. Do that, and see what happens."

Well, we were all listening to this with our jaws hanging open. Attack Art Forester? Might as well talk of attacking Jack Dempsey who, as heavy-weight champion of the world, was well known by every Prince Albert kid as a ruthless killer in the ring. When his father had gone, we hastily counselled Nigel to pay no attention to the advice. Nigel agreed.

Well, the very next day, when two or three of us were in the Spencer backyard and Nigel was playing with one of his snakes, along came Art. He stopped, looked around to make sure no adult was present, and came in through the back gate. We all tensed up. Art always made other kids tense up.

"What ya doing, Spencer?" Art barked.

"Oh just playing with my snake."

"Snake! You play with those things? I might have known a juicer like you would do anything. Give it to me."

"Why?"

"I know a little game with snakes. You hold onto them by the tail and crack 'em. Breaks their neck slick as anything. Hand it over."

The rest of us little kids watched this thing petrified.

To kill a kid's pet snake! But Art could do it, we knew right well. We'd watched him collect baby frogs out on the shore of the big slough once, put them in a jar of water and set it on the fire to boil.

"No," Nigel said, and put the little snake behind his back.

"What are you talking about?" Art gave the smaller boy a hard shove that sent him over with such force that he let go the snake. Art plunked his big boot down on the reptile's tail and held it there. "Now," he said, "I'll show you how this is done."

He reached down and gingerly took hold of the snake's tail and lifted it up. But before he could crack its neck something hit him in the pit of the stomach like a battering ram. It was Nigel Spencer's head, propelled forward with all the force of his wiry, eighty-five-pound body. All the wind went out of Art and he sat down heavily, releasing the snake which one of us immediately captured.

Before Art could struggle to his feet or even gasp out a startled "What the hell?", Nigel Spencer was on top of him yelling like a mad fiend and pounding away with both fists on the big boy's face. There was a lot of force in those blows, too, and they were doing some damage. Finally Art struggled to his feet, brushed the smaller boy aside and stood glaring at him. The rest of us watched, as the forum crowd must have watched and waited for the lions to pounce on the Christians. We knew it would be murder, but we were helpless to move.

But nothing happened. Brushing off his clothes, Art muttered something like "Jees . . . the little juicer's gone crazy. You should be locked up. I'll get you for this." Then, staring blankly at the blood on his finger that he'd wiped from his nose, he stomped out of the back gate.

The funny part was he never did get Nigel. He threatened often enough, but never actually molested him again.

He was never quite sure just what might happen to him if he tried.

One of the best things about Prince Albert was the bush. It filled every vacant lot, of which there were plenty, and completely surrounded the town. On the south side it was mostly trembling aspen, white birch, choke-cherry, willow, balsam, pincherry, some hazelnut, poplar and Saskatoon berry. North of town, across the Saskatchewan River, were sand plains, with great forests of jack pine, spruce and tamarack. We loved them all.

But mostly we loved the bush south of town which surrounded the big slough. The rushes along the shore were filled with nests of red-wings, terns, pintails, hell-divers, and a host of other birds. The woods back from the shore contained innumerable crows, jays, song-birds, magpies, hawks, and others. There were squirrels and cotton-tails, and weasels of all kinds. And now and then we would even see a moose or a deer.

That big slough! The path to it from town wound through the bush, and as we raced down it in the hot days of July we shed our pants and shirts as we ran, ready to plunge into the water as soon as we hit the shore. Then we would swim and wade out into the beautiful, black, soft, squishy muck that covered the bottom, and plaster the stuff all over our bodies, and make mounds of it on the shore. To this day I don't feel really good in water unless I can sink in nice, slippery, gooey muck up to my ankles.

We'd spend the entire day there, perfectly happy. When we weren't in the water we were looking for birds' nests in the reeds, chasing frogs or salamanders along the shore, eating Saskatoon berries or raspberries, or building huts.

The hut we had in the bush near the big slough was the greatest. It was designed and engineered entirely by Hub, while the work was done by all of us. Even as a boy of twelve

Hub knew everything, and could do everything. At least that's the way it seemed to me. He got none of his information from books, because he never read, and certainly none of it from school, because he played hookey so much.

He had, however, an inborn sense of the practical. He knew how to do things almost instinctively, and he had wonderful powers of observation. He could, for instance, put together anything he could take apart. As soon as he obtained something new, from a bicycle to an old gramophone, he immediately took it apart meticulously, and then put it together again. After which the intricacies of that particular mechanism were locked forever in his mind and he could apply the knowledge to any similar problem.

He was, too, amazingly resourceful. We didn't build the hut out of logs or anything as difficult as that. We built it out of new lumber that we pinched from various construction jobs around the place. (We never stole. That was sinful. We just "pinched".) Anything that wasn't nailed down we considered fair game. This included boards, shingles, tarpaper, nails, two-by-fours, and even little windows from an old chicken-coop that was being torn down. We put them all together, and we had a hut. We even lined it with some beaver-board that somebody was foolish enough to leave out, and that gave a space to store things.

Ah–that hut. It was our refuge, our haven, our own private place. Here we roasted spuds that we'd pinched from gardens on the edge of town, kept our magazines with racy pictures of Theda Bara, and smoked dried leaves. I suppose every boy has smoked dried leaves. They taste terrible. You pick them off the trees–ones on the ground are too moist–and you roll them up in bits of newspaper, being careful to see that stem ends don't puncture the sides. Then you get a box of matches–nothing less than a big box will do–for you must light the cigarette after every puff. Then, oh the taste of musty leaves, ink and sulphur. It burns your tongue, stings your throat and belabours your nasal passages. Wonderful!

We never took girls to the hut. This was our pre-girl period and we wanted nothing to do with them. For we were at the age when girls were mysterious creatures – they were just beginning to bother us, that's what it was – to be acknowledged only by gruff words, pushes, thrown snowballs, and braids dipped in inkwells. In fact, through teasing a girl my career almost came to an abrupt end. We were coming home from school on a cold January day. My coat collar was turned up so that I couldn't see much. The street, naturally, was devoid of cars. We'd been teasing this girl all the way home. I said something to her and she took after me. Looking back over my shoulder to see how close she was, I ran smack into the side of a delivery truck. I bounced back into the snow-bank, bruised but unbroken. A split second sooner, and I'd have been directly in its path. Would have served me right, too.

In winter, the hut was headquarters for our rabbit-snaring enterprise. I don't know why we snared rabbits; we certainly never ate them or used the fur. Perhaps it was just for the fun of being out in the deep, silent woods in winter, finding the rabbits' well-worn trails, and setting our wire snares over them. As often as not, when we came to inspect the snare, a weasel or fox or lynx would have been there ahead of us and demolished our victim.

Or maybe it satisfied that deep, primordial urge to stalk and capture, reminding us that, in terms of the age of man, we are but a few seconds away from that hairy hunter whose life depended upon what he could catch.

And it brought us face to face with a stark and brutal fact of life when we came up against the hermits.

I suppose every town has its mysterious people who appear on the streets at dusk. Men who to kids represent the dark world of mystery and evil. Ours were the hermits.

Sometimes when we'd be playing outside in the evening we'd see them plodding along the middle of the road that came into town from the south – never on the sidewalk – each with a gunny sack over his shoulder. They were dressed in ragged caps with ear lugs, black scarves wrapped around their faces, scruffy buffalo-hide coats tied around the middle with rope, and tattered moccasins. If we felt secure enough, we'd hide behind a garage or a tree in the yard and shout something witty like, "Yeah, hermit!" or "Beaver!" But they never lifted their shaggy heads and turned to look at their tormentors. Just plodded on down the middle of the road. Obviously a wicked pair.

What was inside those lumpy sacks they carried? Something too awful to mention aloud. Babies, maybe, that they'd stolen and killed and were delivering to their master, the devil. Art Forester, who purported to know everything, boasted that he knew what they carried, all right, but he wouldn't dare tell. When pressed he would shake his head mysteriously and wink. When we finally found out, it was more terrible than we'd even suspected.

We arrived at the hut one Saturday morning, Nigel Spencer, Gord Perkins, "Pants" Roberts and I. There had been a light snow in the night and as we ran down the path to the hut we were surprised to see fresh footprints leading up to the door – and none leaving. And what footprints – big, sloppy ones that had been made by big, sloppy moccasins, obviously. Curling lazily from the stovepipe that stuck out the side of the hut was a thin coil of smoke. Somebody was in our hut.

In a hurried whispered conference, we decided against running the mile back to town for help in favour of sneaking up and peeking in our little window. Pants Roberts (he got his nickname because he always wore his father's cut-down army pants that bustled in the back scandalously) was finally persuaded to sneak up first. I think we used the specious argument that since he was the shortest he'd be the less likely to be seen. Anyway, he went, while the rest of us stayed back on the path, shivering from the 20-below temperature and ordinary funk.

Pants made it up to the hut all right, and peeked in the window. But he was so absorbed or horrified by what he saw that he neither signalled for us to come nor returned to tell us. Finally, after gesticulating wildly to him, we managed to summon up the courage to follow him. Pants pointed to a small space that was clear of frost to which we could apply our eyes. Gord Perkins looked first, and we had to pull him away so that Nigel could see. Like the others, Nigel made no comment but motioned me to take my turn.

At first I couldn't see a thing because the light outside was so much greater than that inside. But by shading my eyes with my mitts I finally made out two dim figures. The hermits! They'd taken off their huge coats and their caps with the ear lugs and were sitting close to our little heater. Their gunny sack lay on the floor beside them, and from it they were taking something more horrible than a dead baby–garbage. Bits of frozen meat and bread and vegetables, dirty, miserable stuff that they were heating on the stove and devouring ravenously.

But it was the look of the men themselves. Without their coats they were so thin and dirty as to make one weep. The smaller was no more than fifteen years old, judging from his form and manner, but his face was that of an old man. I turned away. I couldn't look any more.

The four of us turned and walked down the path. No one spoke. We'd never seen destitution like that, and it shook our nice safe sense of security. This was what could happen to people, and did. Many a night I lay in my bed and saw the withered, chapped-lipped, scabby, rotten-toothed face of that boy. I can see it still.

The hermits never stopped at our hut again, although

we left food in the hope that they would. Evidently they had been overcome with hunger and cold, and stopped there to rest before continuing their long trek to their own miserable home in the bush. We often saw them on the road, on their way to and from the restaurants down town, from whose garbage pails they grubbed their food. But we never yelled at them any more.

9 *Never Sleep Three in a Bed*

People often say to me–"How lucky to be raised in a big family." The comradeship, love, warmth of the family circle–give and take–outings together. Okay. That's true enough at times. But there are other things, too, like fights and arguments and humiliation and frustration. I don't say I'm unlucky to have been raised in a big family. I wouldn't have changed it. I know those seven other characters helped develop my personality–the good and the bad of it, the strong and the weak. And who but a fool would want to change the way he is?

One thing certain, life was never dull. Just holding your own with that bunch–surviving–required endless versatility and stamina.

Betty was born in 1922, and for a few years after she was able to sit up in a high chair, ten Braithwaites sat down at table for every meal.

And what meals they were! I always thought my father to be a most quiet man, but then I rarely saw him except at meal time, and there was always so much yammering from us kids that no adult had a chance to say anything.

There was one cardinal principle to which most of us were true–never do anything that anybody else wants you to.

A simple request like "Pass the salt" would bring a

snarling rejoinder. "Why should I? It's just as close to you as it is to me."

"It is not."

"Is so."

"Just measure and you'll see!"

Dad sat at the end of the table and Mother at the foot. Ranged along each side, in order of age, were the rest of us. The biggest boys, being the eldest, were up beside Dad; then Doris and Phyllis, Hub and me; Betty and Denny, the youngest, on either side of Mother.

Nobody could lift a fork until Dad said Grace. He would drop his head and mumble, and we would all lean forward trying to catch what he said. In all the years I ate with him I never made out a word of it. I strongly suspect he was petitioning the Lord to get us through one more meal without casualties.

Then he would begin dishing up the meat and potatoes. Always meat and potatoes. More often than not, the meat was round steak, which must have been a lot cheaper then than it is now. Certainly it was a lot tougher. Before frying, Mother would belabour it for half an hour with the sharp edge of the butcher knife, but it had little effect on its leatheryness. There were boiled carrots sometimes, usually pickled beets, and often turnips. Those were the vegetables that we could grow, and that would keep.

Usually there was onion gravy on the potatoes. We consumed great quantities of fried onions in our house. (I was intrigued to learn recently that scientists have now discovered fried onions prevent the collection of cholesterol in the blood vessels. Interesting.)

Denny and I wouldn't eat the onions, of course, so Dad had to painstakingly strain them from our helpings. Mother was great for cabbage salad, too, and Denny wouldn't eat that either. Said it was poison. So the rest of us would try to persuade him to eat it, and there would be a fight. For along with our absolute refusal to be persuaded of anything, each of us was an indefatigable persuader of others.

No matter how furious the fighting became, Dad hardly ever interfered. Not so with Morley. "Look out, now," he would yell when the racket became too loud, "or I'll reach out!" Reaching out was not just an idle threat, either. He had a long arm and a hard hand, so that when it made contact with the side of your head you knew that you'd been hit.

Since Dad dished everything from in front of him, an equal distribution of food was difficult. Each kid would hang onto the plate handed to him until he could ascertain whether or not the next one coming would be larger. Thus we developed strong grips. And since the first to finish was also the most likely to get a second helping, we all became fast eaters. Otherwise, you stood the risk of being undernourished and small – like the runt in a litter of pigs.

There was rarely anything left for second helpings, however, for Dad never did develop that fine sense of proportion that would make everything come out even. Often as not he ran short before he dished his own plate. Then he would look forlornly down the table and say, "Whoops – seem to be a bit short here." Trying to get any food back from the rest of us would be equivalent to putting your hand in a tiger's cage at feeding time. No wonder he was a lean man.

When the first course was finished one of us would look expectantly at Mother and chant, "Puddin er pie er fruit?" Sometimes there was Saskatoon berry pie, or chocolate pudding, which we always called "blamonge". (It wasn't until years later that I discovered that "blamonge" is white pudding from the French "blanc mange".) Sometimes there would be apple pie, but the great days of the barrels of apples from Ontario were past, and apple pie was seen only on special days.

There was much laughter at our table, too. Usually it came after the meal was finished, and the older ones were having their tea. Mother had a good Irish wit, and she was full of stories. She would advise us, for instance, to be sure to learn to cut our fingernails with our left hand in case we lost the right one.

Denny and I laughed easily, often at nothing. I think the worst of all the bad things about growing old is that you lose the capacity to laugh at little things. We would go to church and giggle so uncontrollably at the antics of the choir conductor that we'd have to leave. We'd kill ourselves over some secret joke at the table until Doris would be ready to scream. Laughter – that's what being a kid is.

And competition? Supposed to put mettle in your soul. Well, we had plenty of it.

For example. In a big family, treats are doled out by the parents carefully and exactly, so that each kid will get precisely as much as the others. If they don't, there is a battle. All right, each kid has got his chocolate bar, or his seven jelly beans, or his two and a half cookies. He then proceeds to eat them. But there is always one kid who just *pretends* to eat his (this could be a girl, usually is). He hides it, waiting until all the others are finished. Then he produces it, and slowly, tantalizingly, eats it in front of the others. He'll never share it, of course, because that would be unfair. After all, everybody had an equal amount to begin with. This little game, known as "making jealous", is guaranteed to start a family row at any time.

Then there is the question of older brothers and sisters. Since there were no multiple births in our family, everybody but Morley, the oldest, and Betty, the youngest, had siblings both older and younger than themselves. It's hard to say which is worse. Older siblings are teasers while younger ones are teasees. I'll begin with the teasers.

My older brothers were champion teasers. I was exactly

the right number of years younger than them to be a safe target. I was too small to be able to retaliate physically or mentally, and big enough to make the game worthwhile. Somehow they managed to keep me in a bad temper most of the time, and on the constant verge of hysteria.

There was the occasion, for instance, when I spilled the milk. Since Old Rosie, bless her soul, gave more milk than even we could consume, Mother used to sell a couple of quarts daily to the Branions, who lived near the school. It was my job to deliver it in a large honey pail with a handle and lid. It was a chore I hated. There I was, toting that damned red honey pail, while the rest of the kids were carrying hockey sticks, or knocking each other on the head with dome crackers, or playing "chase" with marbles.

One winter day, when I was just about late for school and hurrying through the short-cut path, I slipped on an icy spot and fell. Both my hands went up in the air, the milk pail flew high, the lid came off, and the whole white, sticky mess came down on top of me. It was the last straw. Howling with anger and humiliation, I ran all the way back home and into the kitchen, where I told Mother the whole dismal story, my tears of rage increasing with the telling.

It was then that a big brother appeared on the scene. For some reason he hadn't gone to high school that morning, and arrived in the kitchen just as I hit the high point of my story. I've got to admit it was the perfect opportunity, and he made the most of it. Smiling benignly upon me, he said, "Cheer up, old chap, there's no use crying over spilt milk!"

Then he took off up the stairs with me after him—screaming and swearing and throwing everything I could lay my hands on. He barricaded himself in the bathroom, jeering back at me as I kicked the door, threatening every reprisal known to man. I knew, of course, that I would never carry out any of my threats. There's an unwritten law in all big families that an older brother will run from a smaller one when the latter has become flaming mad. It's much the same sort of thing as a great dane permitting itself to be chased off a poodle's yard. A kind of property right. But just as it would be suicide for the poodle to pursue the dane any further than its own boundary or to attack it, so would it be folly of the worst kind for a smaller brother to actually try anything on a larger one.

As a kid I was a notorious mitt-loser. One reason for this was that I liked to read while I walked, and since I always seemed to be delivering newspapers, I had plenty of opportunity to do so. So, as I trudged down the streets with the bag of *Prince Albert Heralds* on my back, I'd be reading the latest wire news on something like the Dempsey-Firpo fight.

And here I must digress a bit, to talk about how fascinated Prince Albert kids were with world sporting events.

It is often assumed that because there were no radios or televisions in 1921, we didn't know what was going on in the world. This is totally wrong. There was still the telegraph, which could bring us blow-by-blow, or pitch-by-pitch accounts of heavyweight championship fights or world series ball games.

It is the boxing that I remember best. Every kid in Prince Albert knew all about Jack Dempsey and hated his guts. This, of course, was all due to the great publicity campaign developed by his handlers. By making Dempsey the most hated fighter in history they assured a big gate for his fights against Sir Galahad-type challengers. They did everything possible to discredit the champ. His war record was doubtful. He was a killer, an inhuman monster in the ring. Why he even looked like a killer, with his three day growth of beard (he retained it to prevent bleeding, but we didn't know that), his surly attitude with the press, and the unfair way that he bashed his opponents about.

Well, Dempsey signed to fight Georges Carpentier of France, and I'm sure no sporting event since the days of the Roman gladiators received more publicity. Every day the sports pages were full of it. Carpentier had everything that a Galahad should have. He was handsome, lithe, graceful, modest, clean-living, loving to his mother–and brothers, too, for all we knew. He was smaller than Dempsey, but fast. So fast–I can remember the exact quote–that he could "catch a wild hare". And he was reputed to have a right-hand punch that could flatten a bull.

We all loved Georges and hated Jack. During the entire spring of 1921 we talked of little else. We staged impromptu boxing matches on the street in which the hero, Georges, always clobbered the rat, Jack. Nobody wanted to play the villain role, of course, and so we had to take turns. Many a kid was content to go home with a bloody nose or thick ear because once again the ogre had been bested.

We followed all the press reports. By the night of the fight, on July 2, we knew that close to a hundred thousand fight fans, many of them women, would crowd into Boyles thirty-acre field in Jersey City, and pay well over a million and a half dollars to watch the "Manassa Mauler" finally get his come-uppance. There was no doubt that Carpentier would win. Why, didn't he represent right and goodness and virtue, and didn't those things always triumph in 1921?

On the night of the fight, half of Prince Albert filled the street in front of the *Herald* office. From an upstairs window a strong-voiced reporter, using a megaphone, relayed the blow-by-blow account to us as it came in over the wire. It was a festive occasion–men in straw hats, women in long dresses, kids in bare feet. The popcorn vendor, who usually sold his wares at Central Avenue Park during band concerts, had arrived with his cart and was doing a good business. Enthusiasm was so high that at least two fist-fights got going before the main bout, and there were three dog-fights. O. J. Parsons, a mean enough man to be the only Dempsey fan in town, bet Jim Sheldon, the livery stable operator, that Dempsey would win. But he was the only one to harbour such a treacherous thought.

The fight? Well, it's history. Dempsey demolished Carpentier in four rounds, and smashed the poor chap up so badly that it was rumoured that he'd never fight again. Dempsey went on demolishing opponents until he ran into Gene Tunney much later, and was himself pretty badly smashed up. And because of that–such is the whimsy of fight fans–he became the most popular ex-heavyweight champion of all time!

Where was I? Oh yes, the story of the mitts. Well, as I walked around my paper route, reading the sports page, or the syndicated column of that funny writer, Stephen Leacock, or the adventures of Mutt and Jeff, I would tuck my mitts under my arm so that I could better turn the pages. This same motion also caused me to drop my mitts into the snow, and by the time I noticed they were gone it would be too late to find them. I'd never admit it when I got home, though, because of the roasting I'd get from my brothers.

Once, however, I forgot. I took my mitts to school, I put them on the window-sill, and when I went to get them they were gone. It was so annoying. I knew exactly where I'd put them, but they just weren't there any more. Well, foolishly, I came home and repeated this story. The whole family took up the cry, of course, and soon "I took them to school and put them on the window-sill and when I went to get them they were gone" became a chant.

But all of this was nothing compared to sleeping three in a bed. Anyone who hasn't had this experience has no right to say he knows anything at all about the vicissitudes of life. We managed all right in the summer, because then Morley was back in Nokomis working on a farm. But in winter he'd come home, and there just weren't enough beds to go around. Five boys, two beds: simple arithmetic dictated that in one of those beds there had to be three bodies.

Denny or I, being the youngest of the boys, naturally found ourselves low man in the matter of three in a bed. And when you're low in that situation, you are low indeed. All the mattresses in our house were old, and all of them sagged in the middle. This meant that the two bodies on either side rolled towards the middle, and on top of whoever was lying there. There is no torture in the world to compare with the feeling of two heavy, sweaty, snoring bodies on top of you. It causes a desperate madness. You writhe, you squirm, but those two bulks simply cannot be shoved aside. You gasp for breath, you pant, you want to scream. When you do manage to sink into fitful sleep you dream that you are in the circus and the elephant has sat down on you. You awaken to find the reality is even worse.

Frantically, you calculate the time to be endured until you can escape. You know it's only about two in the morning, and you can't possibly get up until six. That's four hours. But in the middle of the night every minute is like two hours in the daytime. So that figures out to four times sixty, which is two hundred and forty hours, and that, times two, is four hundred and eighty hours. So, for the equivalent of twenty days, you suffer, with no chance of reprieve. Because if you do manage to squirm from between those three hundred pounds of blubber, the two bodies immediately merge and there is no way of getting back. You can't sleep on the outside because there are no covers there, and this is winter, you know, and attics are cold in winter.

No, it is a problem without solution. Yet another of those factors that contributes to the moulding of character. All my life I've had recurrent dreams of being crushed beneath tons of earth, or sinking in quicksand, or being trampled by herds of hippopotami. All my life I've had this awful claustrophobia, becoming terribly nervous when anyone stands close to me, or lies close to me. It's blighted my existence, made a quivering neurotic of me, and ruined my sex life. I often wonder how I might have turned out if I'd had a bed of my own. A great wide expanse to spread out on as I pleased–to sprawl and turn and kick, without worrying about anyone. To be uncrushed, unsquashed, unsqueezed. I might have accomplished great things.

I can't leave this chapter without a final word about Prince Albert. What a place it was for kids! Every kid should grow up in a place like Prince Albert. It had everything. Vacant lots. One of the great tragedies suffered by modern kids is they have no vacant lots. All they have is organized playgrounds, where parents or youth leaders or recreation directors supervise and plan their activities. But the vacant lot, especially one filled with bush, belonged to the kids. Why, a parent couldn't even find his way through that labyrinth of paths! And there kids could do the things they liked to do–climb trees, crawl through brambles, make huts, smoke dried leaves, tell stories, experiment with the opposite sex, and nobody ever worried about what they were doing. They emerged from time to time to eat and sleep, or when a bare foot had been gashed on a sharp stone or a thorn. Outside of that, they were on their own.

Terms like "juvenile delinquent" and "child psychologist" hadn't yet been invented. Kids were expected to do things they shouldn't; that was part of being a kid. We badgered adults, and gave them as bad a time as we could. I remember one heart-felt declaration made by a harassed water-deliverer. In effect, what he said was, "Kids in Canada do more damage than the Germans did in the war!"

How about that?

We had figured out a way to open padlocks. You simply flattened one end of a nail, and then twisted it a bit. Inserted into the keyhole of a padlock and wiggled just right, it would open the lock. We did this with the lock on the box that enclosed the tap of the water pipe.

In Prince Albert–and indeed in many other western cities–the waterworks extended only as far as 23rd Street. All the houses beyond that had their water delivered to them by a big water-tank, drawn by a team of horses. The tank was filled at the water pipe.

Once we had unlocked the box we naturally turned the water on and let it run. It ran over the road and the sidewalk and into surrounding basements and made a fine mess generally. When the water-man came, we were on hand to get his reaction. We naturally disavowed any knowledge of who had perpetrated the dastardly deed, and promised to help him find the culprits. That's when he made his deathless remark to us about the relative destructive powers of kids and the Germans.

The term "teen-ager" hadn't been invented, either. And every transgression of kids didn't become front page news, or the subject of a television special, as it does today. Matter of fact, we got no publicity at all.

Those days in Prince Albert were to be the last that the members of our family were all together. Morley became a farmer in Nokomis, Peter went into a bank, and was sent to a tiny town in the bush called Parkside. We saw them only now and then, and missed them sorely. For a big brother, no matter how much he may tease, is still a big brother after all. You can always find new friends, but your brothers and sisters are the only ones you'll ever have.

10 *Saskatoon – the Big Time*

We moved to Saskatoon in the spring of 1924. I was in Grade Six, and had become editor of the room newspaper in our class. I remember a poem one of the kids handed in:

> Maxwell Braithwaite is going away,
> Going away from old P.A.
> Going to a city of noise and din;
> Won't they smile when he walks in.
> He'll have to say please when he wants a dib,
> Or he's likely to get a poke on the jib.

The Wesley Church Trail Rangers group, in which I was still striving for my first badge, gave me a going-away present of a pen and pencil set. I remember it well, for it is the only going-away present I ever received in my life.

It was an important move for us. We left the big house and its stone wall, with the balls stuck on the top with pink plaster. Left the security of owning our house and embarked upon the unknown. I have never felt completely secure about anything since, for 1924 was the year that I came to realize that we were poor.

Actually we'd become poor some time before that, but I never realized it. When Dad had moved his family to Prince Albert, and gone into partnership with the city's leading lawyer, he'd made a wise move. Prince Albert was a booming city and the judicial centre for the entire northern half of the province. So, Dad had bought the big house and settled down to be a prosperous lawyer, and we were all set to live the lives of sons and daughters of a prosperous lawyer.

Then the fickle forefinger of fate wrote and, having writ, moved on. For some perverse reason, the C.N.R. decided to extend its railway line to the town of Big River, eighty-six miles north-west of Prince Albert, and the Saskatchewan government, in its blithering stupidity, decided to establish a judicial district up there. This meant that a good half of the legal business was diverted from Prince Albert, and about half its lawyers became superfluous.

In spite of having eight kids to support, Dad might have survived even that blow, except that he had a couple of other things going against him. For one thing, he was a Conservative in a Liberal province. And Dad wasn't one of your mild, pragmatic, easy-going men in the matter of politics. He was a zealot. He believed that Sir John A. Macdonald ranked only next to God in importance. He'd once shaken the great man's hand at a picnic, and the first vote he ever cast in his life was for Sir John's party in the election of 1891. Everything since that great Conservative victory had been anti-climactic.

Even worse, ever since Saskatchewan became a province in 1905 it had always had a Liberal government. No Conservative party had ever gained power there, but Dad, along with a few others, was determined that it by-gawd would. So he campaigned in the 1921 election and, of course, was on the losing side. This meant that all the little favours and goodies that a provincial government can pass out to lawyers never came Dad's way. Not only did he not become a judge, he never even made King's Counsel.

So there he was. Not enough legal business to sustain

him, no provincial influence to help him, a family of eight to support, no backlog of savings, and he was fifty-six years old. In desperation, he decided to move to Saskatoon. I guess he borrowed the money for the move, I don't know how else he could have got it. He had no influential friends in Saskatoon, no connections of any kind. He simply moved there and opened a law office, and the family got poorer and poorer.

We weren't even honest-poor. We were what my brother once called "sneaky poor". That is, Mother never admitted we were poor. She managed to keep us living in a good house on a good street, even if she couldn't pay the rent. When the landlord couldn't be stalled any longer we of course had to move, and Mother, being a scrupulously honest Methodist, would try to pay off the rent on the house that we had left. Naturally the rent on the current house got behind, so then we had to move again. As a result, we lived in a half-dozen houses in as many years.

Such is the nature of poverty that it takes a child some time to realize it has actually happened to him. Always, he believes there is some sort of backlog, that when his mother says there isn't money for a new coat she means that there is no *immediate money* in her purse, that she can't afford it *now*. He doesn't realize that there is no money, period. That when the rent comes due there is no cash to pay it, and landlords don't wait for their money. They evict people. They are not friendly and kind. They become unfriendly and nasty. That when you haven't money you are in a very, very bad category indeed. Being poor is hard to accept.

Well, we moved into the house at 760 Baird Street and, on the first day of May, Hub and Denny and I set off for Albert School. I remember the day well. It had snowed lightly in the night and we could see our footprints in the green grass of the boulevard along Clarence Avenue.

Going to a new school. Entering a new group. Being an alien. Right off the other kids are suspicious of you. They sidle up to you along the basement wall, "What'syer name, kid? Wanna fight?"

No answer is required to this, and none is given. You just glare back and the two of you stand there, hackles up, until you can think of a decent way to leave.

On our first day at Albert it was wet and cold outside, and all the kids stayed in the basement. The noise was unbelievable. Little kids running around screaming, bigger kids chasing them, screaming. Some kids sitting in the corner, playing marbles. I can still hear the sound of those marbles bouncing off the cement wall. Kids half-way up the stairs, kids on the floor, kids throwing water from the water-fountain, kids crying, kids cheering, kids swearing.

And then – a voice from the top of the long wooden stairs. "Here comes the Old Man!"

Suddenly dead silence. Like one of those stop-action sequences in the movies, where everyone is frozen in mid-motion. The Old Man, the principal of the school, was short and nimble and bald and wore glasses. He hated all kids. He'd come bouncing down those long steps and walk around the big basement room, his eyes daring any kid to make just one move. Just one. If anyone did, he'd get a cuff on the side of the head, and he'd be hauled up those stairs, two at a time, to the principal's office. If nobody moved, the Old Man would stop, glare at us like a sergeant-major glaring at new recruits, and then shout, "All right, everybody outside!" And outside we'd all go, and outside we'd stay until he was back in his office on the second floor. Then we'd filter back, and the noise and running and fighting would commence all over again.

We did, however, have one big thing going for us at

Albert School. That was Hub. Almost immediately, he became the school's leading citizen–not leading *student*– but leading citizen. Albert had a very good baseball team that spring, which led to visions of winning the city championship. Hub was an excellent ball player, and immediately made a place on the team.

As a matter of fact, Hub became so well-known that for quite a while the kids thought our last name was Hub. Thus, they called me "Little Hub", and Denny "Littler Hub".

Ah, I'll never forget that baseball team! Compared to it, the New York Mets, or the Baltimore Orioles are nothing. The pitcher was none other than Cece Fletcher. Who was he? Why just the best that ever was. And the catcher was Kenny McLeod. An all-round athlete if there ever was one. But the greatest of all the members of that great team was Adam Wenninski.

Adam lived on a farm, and often had to do chores. Sometimes he would have to go home first. Then he would arrive at the ball diamond, in one or the other of the school grounds, riding bareback on a horse.

As the schedule drew to a close that spring, with Albert right up at the top, school work was practically forgotten. The greatest rivalry was between Albert and King Edward. Our principal and the King Edward principal were rivals themselves, and each was determined to win. The final game took place in King Edward Park. The game was about to begin. No Adam Wenninski. The entire student body of both schools was there, of course. We were allowed out an hour early, just so we could make it. And then, when the umpire yelled "Play ball!", Adam Wenninski was still missing. Without his big bat, Albert couldn't win. But the game had to start. They were up first, and we got them out without a run. Then we came to bat, but where was our man Adam? Suddenly somebody saw him, galloping full-tilt across the 25th Street bridge. Such a cheer went up as could be heard clear to Clark's Crossing! Adam pulled his horse up, leaped to the ground, seized a bat, and knocked a home run. In all the annals of baseball – never has there been such a dramatic moment.

And in the fall, Albert School had the best soccer team and won that cup, too. And now our principal became a fiend. He wanted everything in sight. He discovered that there was a cup for public school lacrosse that hadn't been up for competition for years. King Edward had that, too. So why not turn our soccer team into a lacrosse team? Same size field, same number of players. No sooner said than done. A little practice, a challenge, and that cup, too, came to Albert School.

But the greatest triumph of all was hockey. What a team we had. Peggy O'Neil (later with Boston Bruins), Mutt Gardner (later with Montreal Canadiens), Curley Kerr (later with the Saskatoon Quakers), brother Hub, Tommy Hunter, and some other lesser players. All you needed then was six good players, and you had a hockey team. Nobody wanted to go off the ice, ever. And we won that league, too.

Of course in Saskatoon then we had the best hockey in the world from which to get our inspiration. The Saskatoon Sheiks were in the Western Canada professional league, along with Regina, Calgary, and Edmonton.

And there never was a greater hockey team. Most of them are in today's Hockey Hall of Fame, as they well deserve to be. There were the Cook brothers, Bill and Bunny, who played on a forward line with Corbet Denenay. Bill Cook was probably one of the most accurate shots in the game, and when he *did* miss the goal, just as likely as not he'd break the boards at the end of the rink. Corbet Denenay was the fastest and slickest skater I've ever seen in fifty years of watching hockey. And there was tough, old bald-headed Harry Cameron on defence, and Leo Reese who, although he possessed only one good eye, could see far too much for opposing forwards. And none other than George Hainsworth in goal. Wow!

The standard way for us kids to get into the game was to go down to the old arena on Saskatchewan Crescent real early. Then we'd hang around the door, waiting for the players to come. "Carry your equipment, Mr. Cook?" we'd beg as the great men came by, and if we were lucky enough they'd hand us their skates and pads, and let us tag along behind while the ticket-taker glowered. Of course this gave us standing room only, but sooner or later we'd notice a seat with nobody in it, and manage to slide our backsides into place.

Half the fun of the game was watching the rink rats sweep the ice and sell peanuts between the periods. Cleaning the ice, they operated with long-handled push brooms. They walked around with a slick, jerky little pushing motion that slid the ice crystals just ahead of them into the path of the wide broom following. It was precision at its best. Then they'd come out with their baskets of peanuts. There were no aisles in the old arena, and the only way to reach the customer was to pitch the bag up from the rink into his waiting hands. Then he'd toss the money down and the seller would pick it up off the ice. Sometimes he'd even catch it.

But the game itself. Such speed and grace! Such stick-handling! It was against the rules to pass the puck forward anywhere on the ice. Only straight across or slightly back, and the puck-carrier couldn't kick the puck. Also, the body-check hadn't been invented. So the players played the game with their sticks and skates. They could skate like the wind, and they carried the puck on their sticks as though it were glued there.

It would be nice to say that because of all this the game

of hockey in the early Twenties was nice and gentlemanly and mild. But it wasn't. It was rough, tough and nasty–as hockey should be. There was plenty of blood on the ice. Fist-fights were frequent, and butt ends, spearing, and all the other neat little tricks were as common then as now. I remember the Regina goal keeper, Red McCuster, whom we Saskatoon fans considered the dirtiest player of all time. He played most of the game on his knees and it was almost impossible to get a puck past him. And if a forward got in too close, he simply and neatly hit him over the head with his long stick.

Saskatoon won the league and played against Victoria in the semi-finals for the Stanley Cup. Never before or since have Saskatoon people been so hockey-crazy. The rink was jammed every night. During one game, I remember, when Hub and I managed to squeeze into two spaces one above the other, I almost joined the players on the ice. Bill Cook and Bunny Cook were executing one of their spectacular rushes down the ice. Just as they hit the defence, Bill flipped the puck over to Bunny, and he drilled it into the net. To a man the crowd leaped to its feet and went crazy. In his enthusiasm, Hub hauled off and hit me so hard in the middle of the back that I went sailing down over the heads of the people in front and landed in the second row from the ice. But I was too happy to care. Our beloved Sheiks had won the game.

But they lost the series. The final and deciding game was tied after three periods. In an overtime period, George Hainsworth caught a stinging shot. It stayed in his glove for a second, and then slid out and dropped over the goal line. The gloom in Saskatoon was as thick as a London fog.

When we couldn't get into the games we listened to them on home-made crystal sets. Hockey broadcasting was just beginning then, and a group of us would gather in somebody's bedroom. One kid would wear the earphones and relay the play-by-play description to the others, who were sprawled around on the bed and floor following every move of the play. And when the Sheiks scored, the bedroom became a circus of kids pounding each other on the back, throwing pillows, standing on their heads, punching each other, and bouncing on the springs.

For hockey was part of our life. All during the long, cold winter we thought of little else. At school we played at recess and noon hour, and after school we played on the open-air rinks. On weekends we played in church leagues. In the evenings we played road-apple hockey on the street corners, under the flickering light of the street lamps. A kid without a hockey stick in his hand was only half-dressed. We'd walk to school doing a series of hockey shots. Shooting an old tin can or a horse turd or a piece of ice. Always shooting, always stick-handling. Hockey.

And that brings me to Charles Dickens and Goofy Hendrickson and the Cratchit's Christmas dinner. I don't know how a kid picks up a nickname like "Goofy". The same way I got tagged "Fat", I guess, and Eugene Ellingson became known as "Puss", and Ernie Roberts became known as "Pants". A whole book could be written about how kids get their nicknames, and why. Anyway, Goofy Hendrickson had picked up the tag, and it stayed with him. He was the only kid we knew who ate crayons, and he had this interesting habit of tattooing himself with his straight pen by running the nib under the skin of the back of his hands and arms. He also swore a lot. His dad worked for Burns and Co. in their stockyard, and swearing was a necessary accessory to his job. Goofy picked up some expressions that even *we* hadn't heard, and frequently used to beguile us with them.

We were in Grade Seven by now. The teacher was Miss Bishop, and she was pretty and I was in love with her. But not the way I was in love with Elva Mawhinney who sat across the aisle from me. Elva was petite and dark-haired, and had the prettiest little mouth you ever saw. Everything about her was pretty. The way she leaned her chin on her fist when she read from the reader. The way she rested her plump pink arm on the desk when she wrote. The way she tossed her dark curls when she turned her head. The way she walked. The way she did everything just sent me up the wall.

Dickens' *A Christmas Carol* was our supplementary reading and, as every teacher since the story was written has surely done, Miss Bishop decided that we would dramatize the Cratchit's Christmas dinner for the school's Christmas concert. Fine. I was chosen as Bob Cratchit, I suppose because he was tall and skinny and I was short and stout. I sure did hope that Elva Mawhinney would be chosen as Martha, because there's one part in the story where she runs into Bob's arms and he kisses her. Yeeow!

But things never work out perfectly in this imperfect world. Elva was chosen to be one of the young Cratchits – you know, the ones that were steeped in sage and onions to their eyebrows. Goofy Hendrickson was the other one, I suppose because he was the tallest kid in the room and looked about as much like a young Cratchit as he did like a jack-rabbit.

The part of Martha? That went to Edna Trumper. What can I say about Edna? She wasn't petite and frilly like Elva, that's certain. She was kind of long and skinny. And she wore a coarse cotton dress, and coarse cotton stockings and boots. She was a fine girl, though, and certainly did fit the part of Martha, but I could never figure why Miss Bishop – in just this one instance – should suddenly resort to perfect type-casting.

Well, you know the Dickens story. It's full of bounce and good spirits, and is everybody's idea of Christmas dinner. Let's face it, Christmas as we know it was invented by Charles Dickens. But our performance somehow lacked some of the necessary verve and enthusiasm. We wandered about the front of the room mumbling our lines and, try as she would, Miss Bishop couldn't inject any life into the performance – especially into that kissing scene.

Let me see – the exact words from the story are, "she came prematurely from behind the closet door and ran into his arms". It doesn't say anything about Bob Cratchit running the other way, or keeping his arms at his sides, or turning his head and blushing red as a sunset, or trying to dodge. None of that is there at all.

"Come now, Max," Miss Bishop would urge. "You can do better than that. Don't be shy."

How could I explain to her that if she'd just put Elva Mawhinney in that part, she wouldn't need to worry about my shyness. She'd have trouble the other way round, I'll be bound. But I couldn't say that, so I rather welcomed the shyness-bit.

Oddly enough, the only one who showed any real feeling for his part was Goofy Hendrickson. He really dug it. Ran around shouting about sage and onions and pinching the other young Cratchit – Elva – and pulling her hair, and making her dimple all over the place. And when they squeezed into the corner together, as the script called for, it seemed to me he squeezed too damned hard.

Then came the actual eating scene. Here, although he has described a Christmas dinner better than anyone else ever could, Dickens thoughtlessly didn't write down any actual dialogue for his characters to speak. Miss Bishop, being no playwright, had not assayed to correct that deficiency.

"Just talk the way you would normally," she advised, not realizing what she was saying. And we did pretty well at it in rehearsals. I said "There never was such a goose cooked," and Mrs. Cratchit cried with great delight, "We haven't eaten it all at last!" and the young Cratchits filled in the script with "yum yum's", and such a deal of smacking of lips as to make even Scrooge blush.

But came opening night. Or opening afternoon, I should say, and something happened to us thespians. As soon as we saw parents and others coming into that school auditorium, we got buck-fever and got it bad. As a result, we all got sort of hopped up and overdid everything. If we were supposed to speak out, we shouted. If we were supposed to walk fast, we rushed. So when I came in through the curtain as Bob Cratchit, and said my bit about "Where's Martha?" and she came to the part where it says, "ran into his arms", she came out of the cupboard like a lioness coming at a zebra. Naturally I took a backward step, tripped over a stool and fell flat on my back.

The whole thing rather fell apart after that. Nobody could seem to remember what to say or where to stand, with the result that we walked over each others' lines, and into each others' persons, and the play was a shambles. There was a rustle in the wings, which I was sure must be Charles Dickens turning over in his grave, but actually was Miss Bishop, trying to whisper directions to us.

The grand dénouement of all this confusion came with the dinner table scene when the goose was brought in. Nobody could think of a single bright *ad lib*, and we all sat there, heads down, utensils moving foolishly as we stuffed forkfuls of nothing into our tongue-tied mouths. From the wings Miss Bishop kept urging, "Say something, say something, say *something*!"

And finally she got through at least to Goofy. His frightened, benumbed brain finally grasped the idea. A big, stupid smile spread across his homely face. He carefully laid down his knife and fork, turned full face to the audience, and yelled: "It's the best sonofabitch goose ever I et!"

11 *River-Bank Follies*

The south branch of the Saskatchewan River runs through the centre of Saskatoon and dominates the city. The part of Saskatoon on the south side of the river, called Nutana, was settled in 1883 by a band of temperance missionaries led by a man named Lake, and that part of the city has been dry ever since. All of the numerous houses in which we lived in Saskatoon were on the Nutana, or dry, side of the river.

The banks on this side are high and steep, and heavily treed with birch, aspen, elm, chokecherry, Saskatoon berry, and box-elder, or Manitoba maple. When we lived in Saskatoon the river bank on the Nutana side was a vast, natural, secret, mysterious playground for kids.

It was interwoven with narrow paths through the underbrush and between the trees–paths that only kids knew. There were clearings deep in the midst of rose bramble bushes into which only kids and rabbits could find their way. There were great leaning, climbing trees into which only kids would venture. There were caves that only a very few kids knew existed. And, best of all, there were patches of Saskatoon berries and chokecherries on which we could gorge ourselves for hours.

On the riverbank we were absolutely free from parents,

and even the cops rarely ventured into its heavy gloom. Even when they did they never saw anything, and heard only the occasional bird call, which was in reality a warning. The river bank, then, was strictly our domain, our Casbah. And here we spent most of our time during July and August, when we had our holiday from school.

Below this forest, along the margin of the river, was the mud bank where low willows grew, and along which the muddy waters of the river swirled with a fast and deadly current. This is where we fished for goldeyes, and ran about naked, and lay on our backs in the sun and wrestled and made catapults, with which to shoot at woodpeckers and cedar waxwings which we never managed to hit.

It was the most relaxed form of fishing imaginable, and the only kind for which I ever had any real enthusiasm. First we would purchase at Woolworths a ball containing one hundred yards of tough white cord. This we would divide up into six lines, each fifty feet long. To the end of each line we'd attach a railway spike and, at intervals of about eight inches, small fishhooks, which we would bait with worms.

The other end of the line was tied to the top of a slim willow gad that we pushed into the river-bank clay, near the edge of the water. We also attached a small harness bell to the gad, so that when it was pulled forward and sprang back the bell would ring.

We heaved the railroad spike, trailing the line and hooks, fifty feet out into the river. Here, it quickly sank to the bottom where the goldeyes lurk. These pretty, silvery fish, with the golden eye, are peculiar to the Saskatchewan River system. Unless they are cured and smoked by a special process (Lake Winnipeg Goldeye), they tend to be soft and full of bones. But it was good fun catching them.

We just lolled around the bank, stuffing ourselves with berries, and waited for the little bells to ring. Then we'd pull in the line and take off the fish, which might be a sucker or a carp or a chub or, if we were lucky, a goldeye. Some days we'd catch a dozen or so and take them up to the residential area, and peddle them door-to-door at two for a quarter. If there is a better way for a kid to spend his time, I'd like to know about it.

We never swam in the river because the current was too strong and treacherous, and besides, at intervals along the bank were huge pipes, through which offal from the kitchen sinks, bathtubs and toilets of Nutana poured into the river.

We often went down to the river bank at night. Darkness was no problem. In our minds we had a map of every winding path, every clearing, every big tree. We'd play hide-and-seek, and cops-and-robbers, and often we'd light a fire and roast potatoes that we scrounged from somebody's garden, crab-apples that we'd got from Mr. Bergen's big crab-apple tree, and, if we were lucky enough to be able to afford some wieners, we'd roast them too. Sometimes we'd discover that a church group or university class would be having a wiener roast in one of the big clearings, and then we'd crawl close and listen to the stories and the singing of *There's a Long, Long Trail a-Winding*, or *The Daring Young Man on the Flying Trapeze.* We'd hear the laughter and the jokes, and we'd feel like Indian scouts spying on the palefaces.

And that's how Bill Grey and I got into trouble.

Bill was a robust Scottish kid whose father worked in the Department of Agriculture at the university. He was full of adventurous ideas, and could run like a deer. He often got teased by the other kids because he'd never steal carrots, and was always talking about things like fair play and sportsmanship. I guess he was the only kid I ever knew who had what you'd call ideals. He also believed the clean mind in the healthy body bit they taught us at Grace Church Sunday School, and he exercised faithfully. The first year I was in Saskatoon Bill was my almost constant companion.

This Friday night in October we had gone down to the river bank. We had a few potatoes and a half-dozen wieners, and we headed for a favourite clearing which was about a hundred yards from the 25th Street bridge. But, as we ran down the path towards it, we saw the flickering of a camp fire and heard voices. Somebody was there ahead of us.

"Shh," Bill admonished in his best Indian scout style. "Let's sneak up on them and see what's going on."

So we did–without making a sound. We managed to squirm right up behind a huge log at the edge of the clearing and, by peering around it, we could see the group on the other side of the fire. But this was no Sunday School or university group who'd come down there for a little innocent fun. These were two guys in their early twenties whom neither of us had ever seen before.

They each had a girl with them, and as I crept closer my heart beat faster. This, I felt, was going to be something quite different from our other spying adventures. I peered cautiously around the end of a log. I recognized both the girls. One of them, I knew, had the kind of "reputation" we had often heard the older boys talking about, although we didn't know exactly what they meant. The other girl was an entirely different type. I knew her quite well for she lived on the street next to us. And now she wasn't saying anything or laughing loudly like the first girl. In fact, she was quite plainly scared.

"I think it's time I went home now, Frank," I heard her say. "My mother will be worried."

"Aw come on now, Ruthie," the young man named Frank scoffed. "Relax. And drink your beer. You've hardly touched it."

"I really don't like beer very much."

He laughed loud. "You will. It grows on you. Come on, drink up and we'll have some fun."

We could see that the other two were already having a

lot of fun. The guy had his arm around Anna and was kissing her, and she was giggling.

"Look at Anna," Frank urged. "She's no spoil-sport. Come on, Baby, let's you and I make some music." He reached out and pulled her over to him. He was a mean one, I could see, and I wished I was anywhere else but where I was. But still it fascinated me. I squirmed ahead to get a better look around the log.

Ruth was struggling with him now as he tried to kiss her. Then he grabbed her hard and pulled her down. She started to yell, and he put his hand over her mouth and slapped her hard on the side of the face.

She began to cry then and looked at him pleadingly. "You're not very nice," she whimpered.

It was then that Bill did the damned fool thing. He jumped to his feet and shouted in his sternest boy-scout-type voice. "Don't you dare strike that girl!"

I jumped to my feet too, and started away from there as fast as I could go. "Come on, Bill," I shouted. "Cheeseit!"

But we weren't fast enough for those two. They leaped over the fire and had us by the scruff of the neck before we could turn around. Frank had me, and the other guy, Roy, had Bill.

They began to rough us up and we kicked and pulled and yelled about what our dads would do if they didn't leave us alone.

Both the girls left as fast as they could go.

"Hey!" Roy shouted. "Wait. What's the idea?"

But they didn't wait, and when the men turned their attention back to us they were in a foul mood, full of beer and frustration.

The language they used to describe us could scarcely be printed, and while they were using it they kept pushing us and pulling us around, cuffing our heads and twisting our arms behind our backs.

"Come on, you guys, let us go," I pleaded. "We weren't doing anything."

"Oh no–just ruined everything, that's what you did," Frank growled. "It'll be the frosty Friday before I ever get that mouse alone again. Damn your rotten little hide." He emphasized his remark by giving my arm an extra twist.

"You chaps will get into serious trouble if you don't release us," Bill advised them, and got his own arm twisted for his pains. He also got a punch on the nose and, as the blood streamed down his face, we both realized that we might be in very big trouble indeed.

"What will we do with these young bastards?" Frank asked.

Roy looked down towards the river. "Well, we could throw them in. That'll cool them off."

"Hey, don't do that!" I was really scared now. "It's deep out there and the current is strong."

The trouble with situations like this in real life is that there's no last-minute rescue. In all stories in books, movies, and magazines, no matter how bad things get for the good guys there is always a dramatic rescue in the last reel or chapter. The bad guys are bested, and the good guys win. So, no matter how terrified or worried or excited you may be about the final outcome, at the back of your mind is the knowledge of this time factor. You *know* that before the ending, good must triumph over bad, right over wrong, the hero over the villain.

I kept listening for the clump of footfalls through the bush that would signal the arrival of help. None came. This was reality, not fiction. As I felt myself being shoved towards that dark and dangerous water I had, for the first time in my young life, the realization that there really was no one watching over me, sheltering me with the great wings of righteousness. I was for it.

Today, when I read of children in African or Asian

villages being threatened by an enemy, either in the sky above or in the jungle around, I get a horribly real feeling of what they must be experiencing. This is it. It's actually here. No rescue. No help. People do kill little children, or hack off their hands, or tear out their tongues, for any number of brutal reasons. We see it happen on television – live, and in glorious colour.

I would like to be able to say that by some daring physical or mental feat we bested, or tricked, or outwitted our captors, but it was nothing as glamorous as that. What saved us was that we began to cry. We cried with sheer, cruel, animal terror. We were afraid of being drowned. We cringed, and whimpered, and begged for mercy. We promised that we'd never tell anybody, and that we'd never do it again – although heaven knows when we'd be likely to get the chance. And it worked. Our complete submissiveness saved us. Just as a big dog won't destroy a cowering little dog, so Frank and Roy couldn't destroy us. They cuffed us soundly and let us go. We were up that dark path like a shot, and long gone from that district before they could change their minds.

I've never felt particularly good or bad about the incident. There is a chance we may have saved Ruth from a pretty rotten time. It may be that she agreed to come to the river bank with Frank from pure ignorance of his type of guy, and the way he was likely to behave, and that she would never take such a chance again. At the time, both Bill and I were too ashamed of our cowardly attitude to talk about it to each other, let alone tell anyone else. The subject just never came up. The standards which had been instilled in us simply wouldn't permit us to face the fact of our poltroonery.

But we quit sneaking up on people, and prying into their affairs.

My brother, Hub, had a thing about pigeons. When we moved to the house on Temperance Street (Mother couldn't stall the landlord on Baird Street any longer), he decided to go into the pigeon-raising business seriously.

"I tell you, Fat, there's money in them," he confided. "They multiply like flies, and once you get them to nest at your house they never go away." He was dead right on the last point, but dead wrong on the first.

He knew where there were some pigeons, too. Unattached pigeons, you might say, that could be had for the taking, for they nested under the arches of the 25th Street bridge.

The 25th Street bridge in Saskatoon is at the end of Clarence Avenue and University Drive, and the main road down from the University. It is built of concrete, with eight piers standing in the river. In between these piers are concrete arches and, if a kid was agile and daring enough he could cross the wide river by running up and down these concrete ramps from pier to pier. There was just one catch: at each pier you had to manoeuvre your way around a narrow ledge in order to get onto the next arch. If you slipped and fell, you'd land on very hard concrete about thirty feet below. There was a dirty brown stain half-way up one of these piers that was, so it was whispered, the dried and weathered blood of a kid who had fallen at some time in the dim past. We would stand and stare up at it, motionless and silent, our young lives momentarily blighted by the realization that all is dust.

Hub, being both agile and daring, often led us across the bridge by the underneath route. It was a great trial for me, because I had acrophobia. When the other kids would climb up telephone poles and slide down the guide-wire to the ground, I just couldn't do it. When they walked along the concrete railing of the bridge–at least two feet wide and perfectly safe–I wouldn't dare. If I got up on anything which was over two feet above the ground, my knees turned to jelly and I had an irresistible urge to jump. I didn't know that I had acrophobia, of course, nor did any of the gang. They and I concluded that I was chicken.

It wasn't until many years later that I discovered I wasn't chicken at all. I was as helpless to combat this affliction as a kid with one leg is to grow another.

This is one respect in which kids today are better off than we were. They *know* a lot more. Every kid today knows about psychology. You hear them talking about their feelings of insecurity, inferiority complexes, paranoia, inhibitions. They understand that when they can't do something another kid seems able to do – there's a reason for it. That it's just as natural for one kid to be more daring than another as it is for one to have better eyesight, or curlier hair. Most adults still cling to such artificial distinctions between people; still feel compelled – for example – to boast of their sexual prowess. But today's kids, when they grow up, won't have such compulsions. They'll be more with it, understand their hangups better, be capable of explaining their own prejudices and bigotry. They won't be so easily conned or persuaded. The world can't help but benefit from such enlightenment.

Anyway, Hub knew that it was under the bridge the pigeons lived and had their nests and this, he decided, would be the source of our pigeon supply.

How do you catch pigeons? They can fly and you can't. Well, pigeons sleep at night, and it's possible, somebody informed us, to capture them then by shining a flashlight on them. They won't move; they'll just sit there like a country boy at Piccadilly Circus, stunned by the bright lights, and wait to be gathered in. Nothing to it.

So we set out at night with a gunny sack and a flashlight to capture the pigeons under the 25th Street bridge. An old board leaning against the first pier served as a ramp, up which we scrambled. From there on it was a matter of running up the arches and making the hazardous traverse of the ledge. Finally we were right up under the roadway of the bridge and we could hear the pigeons restlessly moving above us. To reach them, Hub had to negotiate another ledge that took him out over the river, and fifty feet below we could see the muddy swift water of the Saskatchewan, waiting to swallow us up.

"Hey, Fat . . ." I heard him call in the darkness, "I got a couple. I'll drop the sack down to you."

The sack with two fluttering pigeons fell down on my head. I made a desperate grab to prevent the sack, or me, or both, from falling into the river. I made it, and held the sack until Hub scrambled down from his perch. We had two pigeons.

We took those pigeons home and put them in a wooden box with a wire front, and sat and looked at them. Blueish feathers they had, and pert blueish heads that turned this way and that as they stared at us with their beady eyes.

"God–pigeons!" Hub kept repeating over and over.

We fed the pigeons, and watered them, and watched over them. We gave them good pigeon-names–Pete and Patricia. We built a little house for them that we made secure up under the eaves, with a little door and a little perch outside it. When we thought they'd been with us long enough to feel at home, we transferred them from the pen to the house, with the hope that they'd take up housekeeping. They flew away and never came back.

So it was back to the 25th Street bridge for more pigeons. The next pair we got were even prettier than the first. Instead of being blueish, they were bronze, with streaks of white running through them. "I'm glad the first two didn't stay," Hub opined with the simple logic of expediency. "This pair is better."

We went through the same process. Exactly the same,

right up to the part where they flew away and never came back.

It was then that we realized that keeping pigeons wasn't going to be as simple as we'd supposed. The hard part wasn't getting them; it was keeping them. We fed them better, and kept them penned up longer. With each pair we stood and watched anxiously to see if they might condescend to stay. And each pair flew away.

How *do* you get a pair of pigeons to stay? Actually, it turned out to be quite easy. On one of our forays Hub discovered a pair of half-grown pigeons in a nest. Acting on impulse, we brought these home instead of adults. We gave them a soft, downy bed, fed them soft foods and acted as Mother and Father to them. Sure enough, when they were finally able to fly they didn't even try to leave us, but built a nest up under the eaves. We had our two pigeons.

Then we learned something else about pigeons. They multiply fast, and they never leave the place where they were raised. Our pair reared two offspring, and they in turn reared two more, and it was wonderful. The soft cooing of birds on the roof, the rapid flutter of wings, the sight of them alighting in the neighbour's garden and pecking out his seed peas–all of these joys were ours. Unfortunately, our landlord again lost patience, and again we had to move, leaving our beloved pigeons behind.

Years later, when I was far removed from Saskatoon and my boyhood and had kids of that age myself, I returned to look at the house on Temperance Street. There it was–the caragana hedge, the tiny front lawn, the glass front door through which I'd once shot a hockey puck–and the pigeons! They practically covered the place. Brown ones, black ones, white ones, bronze ones. There was also a tattered "For Sale" sign, tacked to the verandah post.

I spoke to a man who came out of the house and told him I might be interested in buying the place.

He was unimpressed. "Nobody will ever buy this place."

"Why not?"

"Pigeons!" He went black in the face. "Those bloody pigeons! They've ruined the place! They've ruined the whole street!"

"Uh–don't you like pigeons?"

"Sure. One pigeon–or two–or even a dozen. But not thousands! We have pigeons the way other people have mice. You can't sleep at night for pigeons. You can't step out on the verandah without stepping in pigeon . . . ."

"I wonder how they came to settle here?" I asked innocently.

"I just wish I knew. I just wish I knew. If I had the guy who first brought pigeons here I'd pigeon him all right."

"You don't own this house then?"

"This place? I hope to tell you I don't. I can't even stand it as a renter–even with houses as scarce as they are! I'd rather live in a shack. I'd rather live in a tent. Pigeons!" He stomped off down the street.

12 *Masturbation is the Thief of Time*

We learned about sex in the gutter, and as far as I'm concerned that's the best place to learn it. One thing about being instructed in the pleasures and hazards of sex by our peers was that they, at least, were honest. They may have been a bit mixed up here and there on some of the more technical points, but no other kid would ever deliberately lie to me regarding such matters, which is more than I can say for the adults.

I guess the 1920's could be described as the last decade when sex was still under a rock. At least it was with my parents, my teachers, my boys' club leaders, and just about every other adult I met. They were all too religious and decent and refined to talk honestly about anything as nasty as sex.

But we kids now, we talked about it frankly all right. In fact we talked about little else. We had an endless supply of dirty stories that we'd tell while sitting under a lamp post, or loitering in a cave, or resting our backs against a house somewhere. Most of them featured newly-married couples: "Hey, have you heard the one about the bride whose nightie got starched before the wedding night?"

"No, how does it go?"

"Well . . . you see . . . ."

As ten- and twelve-year-olds we sure knew an awful lot about what went on in conjugal bedrooms.

We dug a cave in the willow bush out at the end of our street. Three rooms it had, connected by tunnels ten feet long. What a cave! Brother Hub planned and supervised the work from beginning to end. It was at least eight feet deep, and the main room contained a small stove that we'd pinched from behind a garage on Clarence Avenue. And there we'd sit of a fall evening, munching carrots pinched from the experimental gardens of the university, and roasting their best hybrid corn, and smoking cigarettes that Windy Watson had lifted from Macdonald's grocery store where he worked.

Windy Watson–now there was a kid who was hep. He knew more, that kid, than most adults do today. He got his knowledge, as we all did, from experience. His father'd been killed in the war, and his mother made aprons that Windy sold from door to door. He had the best spiel of any kid I've ever heard: "Daddy was killed in the war, you see, and Mummy and I are having a hard time making both ends meet." He would look so sad and forlorn and miserable standing there clutching his pitiful little aprons that no one could resist him. When he'd made the sale and was out of sight he'd chortle to himself, light up a fag, have a few quick puffs and chew some sen-sen before going on to the next house. By working in Macdonald's grocery and selling aprons, Windy practically kept his family, and also managed to have time for the shenanigans that went on in the cave.

I remember when Windy began to show up with expensive presents and Hub, who knew everything, was worried. A big, brown leather catcher's mitt that cost at least twelve dollars was proudly exhibited one day. Another day, a camera. Another day, a new sweater.

"Where in hell are you getting all this stuff, Windy?" Hub wanted to know.

"From Bart."

"Who's Bart?"

"A guy I know. Lives in an apartment down in the Drinkle block."

"Married?"

"Naw. Lives alone."

"Yeah – well, just don't turn your back on him, that's all I've got to say. I'd like to see where that guy lives."

Windy took us to the apartment once, I remember, when Bart was at work. It was well-furnished, with fancy carvings of things and pictures on the wall, and it had a sort of funny feeling about it. I didn't feel comfortable there. Windy showed us some of Bart's magazines with pictures of nudes in them. He even dug out some dirty postcards that Bart kept in a drawer, one of which featured a boy on his knees in front of a naked man.

Hub became even more worried about Windy, but Windy assured him he needn't be. Turned out all right, of course, because when Bart finally got around to what he was after, Breezy just told him to go screw himself. And that was that.

But to get back to the cave. We had some fine times there. Windy kept us supplied with cigarettes, cigars, chocolate bars and other goodies from the store. I don't know why Macdonald never became suspicious of him, but he didn't. In fact, he boasted about him: "That Watson kid is the best boy with customers I've ever had." On Sundays, he let Windy ride the big black mare which, during the rest of the week, pulled the delivery cart, and Windy magnanimously let us have a ride now and then. He was never stingy like a lot of other privileged kids are.

The cave was also a marvellous place to take girls. And, of course, there were girls curious enough to want to go there with us. It was all innocent fun. We learned a few things from them, and they learned a few things from us.

We were too young for anyone to get pregnant, and the adults didn't seem to mind much. I'm sure some of them must have known what was going on, but nobody called in the morality squad.

The room in the cave where we carried out our fumblings was always kept dark – I guess the girls insisted on it – and it was always cool and damp, the way caves are. For a long time afterwards my thoughts of sex were associated with cool, dark places, furtive whispering and giggling, and the fetid smell of girls' drawers.

As I say, our elementary sex education was simple, straightforward and right. It wasn't until we graduated into secondary sex education that things got fouled up. This happened after I entered high school, when I was removed from the straightforward atmosphere of the gutter and came under the influence of adults. I was thirteen years old, and I'm sure that must be the worst time in any boy's life. Thirteen sure is an unlucky number. And whatever guy dreamed that notion up must have been thinking of boys, because my thirteenth year was the worst one of my entire life.

My parents would never speak of sex at all. I'm sure they must have practised it because – well – eight kids, but they certainly never recognized it in any other way. Once, while rummaging in my dad's dresser, I came upon a brown book that was so old the pages were yellowing, and the spine had been broken so that the book was really in two halves. Faint gold lettering on the scurfy cover said that it was the *Young Husband's Guide to Married Sex*.

What a guide! Naturally I pored over it, and naturally I was baffled. The language was incomprehensible and the advice was ridiculous. There were no illustrations, the print was tiny and faded. As I sat there on the edge of the big bed where all of us children had been conceived, stealing this surreptitious look into the forbidden world of erotica, my father came into the room and stood tall and silent before me. Without speaking, he took the book from me and replaced it in the drawer. Then, still not talking, he took another book from another drawer and, without looking directly at me, placed it in my hands. "Here, I guess you're old enough to read this."

As one looks back over one's life, certain people and events stand out as having a profound effect on one's future. Such an event was the discovery of this old, old masterpiece. It was called *The Solitary Vice,* and it scared the bejesus clear out of me. I still get horrible feelings of guilt and fear, and my brow starts to sweat, just thinking about it.

The writer of *The Solitary Vice* had the most graphic style of any writer I've since encountered. He described the terrors of masturbation as they've never been described before. Compared to it, leprosy, rabies, bubonic plague, syphilis even were no more than slight aggravations. I can't think of one catastrophe that wouldn't befall the practitioner of this awful crime. He would go blind, insane, hairy-palmed, impotent, until he cried out in his misery, "Oh who will deliver me from the body of this living death?"

I sat there on the edge of that bed, and the sweat poured off me in buckets. I have never been so terrified of anything in my life. Of all the good things my father did for me–and he did plenty–he came close to wiping them all out by placing that awful book in my hands.

I couldn't sleep, I couldn't eat, I dreaded being alone, I prayed long and earnestly to be saved.

Just about that time, too, I came under the influence of the drill and hygiene teacher at high school. He was a fine man, I suppose one of the finest in the city. He was tall and straight and hairy-chested and frightfully religious. He didn't drink or smoke or fool around with women. He was without doubt the leading boys' worker in the city, being the head of the largest boys' club. He was absolutely full of good advice to boys, and constantly lectured us on the virtues of honesty, manliness and good sportsmanship, "play up, play up and play the game".

And he was never more vehement and earnest than when lecturing us on sex. Since we were segregated from the girls for these classes he could be perfectly frank. I can still see him standing up there in front of the class, jaw out-thrust, eyes flashing, warning us of the dangers of losing our manhood. He was far too decent a man to use words like masturbation, of course, but he made his meaning clear, all right. He told us about capons, for instance, and steers and geldings who had all their masculinity taken from them by the removal of their "vital parts", and he made it clear that we could destroy our own manhood by indulging in sinful practices.

While he was at it, he warned us of the dangers of having anything to do with girls. Plenty of time for that later in life, he said, but now there were more important things to be done. He instructed us in methods of sublimating our sex drives (never using the words, of course) by playing hard and working hard. "Take it out in good manly sports–such as boxing, wrestling, club swinging, rugby and the rest." I was so ashamed I couldn't look at him.

He had a tremendous influence on the young, that drill teacher. On weekends he would take boys on hunting and fishing trips, and after church he always had a group of his favourites come to his home–he lived with his mother. Here, they would discuss deep and religious matters. Some of the boys would even stay all night and sleep with him. The devotion and dedication of this wonderful man is something you rarely see in teachers today.

I never went to his home after church, or on any of his hunting or fishing trips. I was too ashamed. For I had the solitary vice. God, how I had it! Each day I inspected my hands for signs of hair; every night I prayed to be spared the horrors that I knew lay in wait for me.

My situation was made worse by the fact that I was alone so much of the time. Each evening, right after school, I tore down the short hill, across the old traffic bridge, north along Third Avenue to 20th Street and the office of the *Star-Phoenix*. There, I loaded a hundred and twenty-five papers on my back, trudged back across the bridge and began delivering my route, which took me up to Eighth Street. A couple of hours later I staggered into the house, tired and hungry.

It was during those two hours that I had my worst times. Nothing to think about but sex. Not the girls in my room at school – I was shy with them – but Clara Bow and Norma Shearer. Clara Bow – you dimple cheeked, round-assed little devil you! I could hardly walk for thinking of Clara Bow.

To alleviate my condition, and keep my mind off Clara Bow and my hands off myself, I began to memorize the poems of Robert Service. "The Cremation of Sam McGee" came first, and then "The Shooting of Dan McGrew". Then I got *Rhymes of a Red Cross Man* and learned "Bill the Bomber", "My Foe", and "The Wee Penny Whistle of Sandy McGraw". The rhythm of Service's poems just suited my stride, and as I walked back and forth along 12th Street, 11th Street, 10th to Main, 9th and 8th I recited them to myself.

Rarely, if ever, have the poems of Robert Service been recited with more determination and conviction. Dan McGrew died a thousand deaths as I trudged along the streets with fifty pounds of papers strapped to my back.

Indirectly, I suppose, I owe a lot to that solitary vice and the poems it inspired. Every Friday evening at high school, we had a meeting of the literary society, or as it was generally called a "lit". Talent was always in demand, and one night I found myself on the stage reciting, with appropriate gestures, "The Cremation of Sam McGee". At first I didn't do so well, but when I began marching back and forth across the stage with the same stride as I used on the street, the whole performance gained style and momentum. The audience, who had never seen a striding reciter before, thought it was something new and gave me a big hand. After all, if a bagpipe player can walk, why not an elocutionist? Henceforth I was known as "the roving reciter".

Once on the stage I couldn't get off. The applause of the crowd infected my mind like a virus. After that, I would leap onto the boards and ham it up at every possible opportunity. From that came writing skits, and from that, other types of writing. Who says there's nothing good to be said for masturbation?

It was just about this time, too, that I discovered pornographic literature. I didn't have to hide it under my mattress or in a dark closet. It was perfectly legitimate and respectable, bound in a big brown volume, written by that master pornographer, William Shakespeare.

Because we were still poor, purchasing textbooks was a major problem. I think the play in the Grade Nine course of study was *King Henry IV* and, since I didn't have a proper text, I began searching through the bookcases for a copy of the play.

Our house was full of bookcases. My father was a great lover of books, and in his more prosperous days had spent thousands on them. There were sets of books in those cases that I've never seen anywhere else. The complete Mark Twain, for instance, and a whole shelf of books containing all the works of Alexander Dumas. A famous set of travel books, full of beautiful pictures on glossy paper, called *Stoddard's Lectures*, with captions on the pictures like "A Thing of Beauty" or "A Characteristic Cascade" or "A View from Murren." A set called *The Makers of Canada* and another, in twenty volumes, with each book distinctively bound, which was called *The Great Events by Famous Historians*. There was also a book entitled *Modern Eloquence,* containing speeches by Mark Twain, William Jennings Bryan, and countless other great orators. It was from these that I cribbed speeches for boys' banquets, and thus gained something of a reputation as an eloquent chap.

Among the shelves of books I found two complete works of Shakespeare. One was small and dainty, bound in padded black leather covers, with gold lettering on the outside and the smallest conceivable print on the inside. It was a present from Dad to Mother in 1897, four years before they were married. The other was a hefty brown volume, which contained all the plays, all the sonnets, all the poems, and copious notes. I carted this "big brown book" off to high school, where it caused me no end of embarrassment.

For the book wasn't the censored, watered-down version that appeared in the high school texts. The plays were there exactly as first printed, with all the good round oaths and lusty references intact. It was the custom of Miss Ranken, our teacher, to have us read the parts in the plays, and it was a source of great amusement to the other kids when I read about whores and whoremasters and the like. We'd be droning out the words in our Saskatchewan version of Shakespearese when I'd come out with a line like, "Why, thou clay-brained guts, thou knotty-pated fool, thou whoreson, obscene, greasy tallow-ketch – "

Everybody would stop and look at me. Miss Ranken would blush and try to pretend she hadn't heard it, and Bill Reid or some other wag would put up his hand and innocently enquire, "Please, Miss Ranken, I can't find that part about whores in my book."

"Never mind, just go on reading."

The first time it happened, Miss Ranken asked to see

my book and, after glancing through it, suggested that perhaps I'd better get an authorized text. But I never did.

The big brown book had a much more devastating effect on my delicate young mind, however. One day as the class was ploughing its way through a scene and I had no part to read, I idly turned over to the back of the book, and began reading at random from one of the poems. This was the line that hit me:

"He on her belly falls, she on her back."

Holy prozotsky! I just about went up through the ceiling. A description of sexual intercourse right here in a book–a legitimate book!

Hurriedly I thumbed back to the beginning of the poem. It was "Venus and Adonis" and right from the beginning it was perfectly plain that this beautiful, voluptuous, naked goddess of love was doing her best to seduce this beautiful youth, also naked. Man! This has got to be the sexiest situation in literature. Here she was, panting after the boy, using every wile in the female arsenal to get him to respond. Wow! Such imagery!

'Fondling,' she saith, 'since I have hemmed thee here
Within the circuit of this ivory pale,
I'll be a park, and thou shalt be my deer;
Feed where thou wilt, on mountain or in dale:
Graze on my lips, and if those hills be dry,
Stray lower, where the pleasant fountains lie.'

On and on I read, going hot and cold by turns, panting as even Venus herself did pant. Yowee! Verse after verse of the same thing. It was almost more than the flesh could bear.

So absorbed was I with the problems of this beautiful goddess and her reluctant swain that I didn't notice the stumbling voices around me had become stilled. In fact a complete silence had descended upon the room, and gradually, through the mist of erotica clouding my brain, this fact became apparent to me. I heard Miss Ranken's voice, as unlike Venus's sweet tones as any voice could be, ". . . Max, I asked you what you are reading!"

"Um . . . mm . . . what?"

"It must be very absorbing. I've asked you the same question three times and you haven't even heard me."

"Well . . . uh . . . just . . . uh . . . Shakespeare."

"Indeed. We'd all like to share it. Perhaps you could read it for us."

"This? No . . . Miss Ranken . . . really, I couldn't."

"If you please."

"Uh . . . which part of it?"

"Right where you're reading will be satisfactory."

"Out loud?"

"We could scarcely hear it otherwise."

"Well . . . okay . . . ."

And I started to read:

Now is she in the very . . . uh . . . lists of love,
Her champion mounted for the hot encounter:

But that's as far as I got. Bill Reid let out a low whistle. Somebody else shouted "Wow!" and started to applaud. Miss Ranken came skidding down the aisle, snatched the big brown book from my desk and glared at it. Then she slammed it shut and plunked it on her own desk, very red of face and flustered. Mercifully the bell rang then and the class filed out of English in high glee. Later, I got my book back, and no more was said of it.

But it wasn't the end of it for me. I had dipped into the font of vicarious, erotic delight, and I was ready for the complete plunge. From the pastoral eroticism of "Venus and Adonis" I went on to "The Rape of Lucrece", with all its dark, foul, lust and evil-doing. What an epic of tragedy that was, written to arouse erotic feelings in the youthful Earl of Southampton.

Full of robust lines like:

By reprobate desire thus madly led,
The Roman lord marcheth to Lucrece' bed.

and –

His hand, as proud of such a dignity,
Smoking with pride, march'd on to make his stand
On her bare breast, the heart of all her land.

and –

For with the nightly linen that she wears
He pens her piteous clamours in her head.

Now I want to tell you that's gutsy stuff. Rough, ragged, randy rape, it was. And she having lost "a dearer thing than life", after fourteen stanzas of doleful lament summons her husband home, tells him all, and kills herself.

We are told that Shakespeare wrote these two poems in 1593 and 1594, while the Plague was ravishing London and there was little doing for actors, to establish himself as a literary man – a thing he could never accomplish by writing plays for the vulgar multitude. And we are also told that the poems were immensely popular, ran into numerous editions, and were greedily read by the young bloods of the day.

I got the big brown book out the other day, re-read both poems, and was struck by the difference that forty-four years can make. Now, a thirteen-year old can go into any bookstore and buy a copy of *Lady Chatterly's Lover, Fanny Hill, Candy* or *Cocksure,* or any one of a dozen sex-thrillers, and read all about the most intimate details of sexual intercourse. He doesn't have to wade through verses of high-blown poetry to get to the good parts. It's all there, spelled out in good old-fashioned Anglo-Saxon four-letter words.

But is it any more erotic? Is the exact description of sex any more stirring that the poetical hinting at it? Is the bikini more stirring than a glimpse of an ankle? I remember when Clara Bow appeared in a bathing suit she was pretty well covered from neck to knees. And she drove me to madness. But was she really more sexy than Bridget Bardot dressed in nothing? Or was I just more excitable in those days?

Perhaps I have dwelt too long on this puberty thing, but it's one of the most vivid impressions that remains from my first year in high school in Nutana. Another unforgettable memory is the first Field Day, and how our dog Pal and I disgraced ourselves, the family, and the school.

13 *The One-Hundred-Yard Schlemozzle*

Of all the dogs that have gone squirming, tail-wagging, and yapping through my boyhood, Pal was the most memorable. He was the nuttiest, most affectionate, stubbornest, fightingest, most intelligent dog I ever knew. And my brother Denny and I loved him completely.

He was really Denny's dog. He'd got him the way we always got dogs, that is by having the dog adopt us, rather than by us making any overt move to acquire it. Pal belonged to an acquaintance of ours, and when they went on their summer holidays in 1926 they paid Denny a fee to look after him. So he came to live with us, much to the disgust of my sister, "then-they-say-keep-a-dog Doris", and my mother who was having a hard enough time to feed us, let alone a fussy dog.

Pal was a small, whitish dog whose long fur was constantly smirched and filled with burrs. In general conformation, he resembled a collie. That is he had a long nose, long hair, a long tail and was rather lean. We used to describe him as "a pure-bred white Scotch collie who has been stunted by distemper." And I guess that's a good way to leave it.

As to characteristics. He liked to fight, to chase cars, to dig in people's gardens (the better the garden, the better he liked it), and to eat Mother's baking-powder biscuits. He didn't like to swim, to do what anyone told him, or to be separated from us under any circumstances.

As a result, he followed either Denny or me or both of us everywhere we went. And since the guiding passion of his life was to get into fights, his presence was a constant embarrassment. He'd follow us into the Daylight Theatre down on Second Avenue, for instance, and hide under the seat. That was fine, unless the picture had a dog in it and that dog should begin to bark. This was the era of Rin Tin Tin, a dog whom we considered to have all the admirable characteristics Pal lacked, and whose fiims we never missed. But when Rinty got after a crook and began to bark, Pal would begin to bark and growl under our seat. Whereupon an indignant usher would come poking about with a flash-light and say, "Where's that dog?" and we'd say, "What dog?" Finally the usher would locate him, drag him screaming up the aisle and pitch him out onto Second Avenue. But in no time Pal was back under our seats, ready for the next encounter.

He followed Denny to school and when the principal tried to put him out Pal bit him. Mother never could forgive this. "Imagine," she would say, "a dog who bites the principal of the school! Has he no respect for anything?" Mother never did like Pal much. Maybe it was because he just about doubled her housework. His long hair was always full of mud and assorted other foreign bodies, which he would leave in little piles around the house, wherever he happened to sit or lie. Often this was on a couch or a bed. He was also covered with fleas, which he generously distributed. Sometimes, when Mother would see Pal lying in the middle of the living room rug, vigorously chewing at fleas, shaking his long, floppy ears and wagging his burr-filled tail, she would sit down and weep.

We rarely gave him a bath because he hated water so.

I've never known a dog to hate water as Pal did. Even taking a drink he would gingerly approach the dish, stretch his neck out as far as he could, then stretch his tongue out to its fullest extent, after which he would cautiously slurp the stuff.

Pal's hatred of water disappointed us more than anything else about him. We had always wanted a dog who would chase sticks into the river, swim out and get them, then turn around and swim back, puffing and blowing as any decent dog should. We knew kids with dogs that would fetch anything–stones, sticks, great branches off trees, rubber tires, anything. And God, how we envied them! But mostly we envied the kids whose dogs would swim in the river.

We spent hours trying to train Pal to go into the water. This at first consisted of pitching things into the water and shouting, "Fetch, Pal, fetch! Good boy, go and get it!" Pal would sit on his backside and look at us as though we were crazy, his long tail gently brushing the river-bank clay. Finally we gave up on the "persuasive" method and went in for coercion. "Go get it, you stupid mutt!" we'd shout, pretending to hit him with our fist. He'd cringe back and look at us with his big brown eyes, but he still wouldn't budge. Finally we picked him up by the paws, me at the front, Denny at the rear, swung him back and forth and pitched him as far out into the muddy water as we could.

But that, too, was a complete failure. He just sat there on the bottom with the current swirling about him and stared at us. Then, looking like a gopher that's been drowned out of its hole, he'd creep out of the water, white hair plastered to his skinny body, stand in front of us and shake water all over us. Then he'd be overcome with an abundance of exuberance and go dashing back and forth among the willows of the river bank like a colt let out of the barn in the spring. Yapping and jumping he'd go and we'd say, "See, he really likes it. We did him a favour."

But if he did really like it, he had the strangest way of showing his enthusiasm. Because after a while he wouldn't come within fifty feet of the river's edge. Instead, he would stay up in the bushes while we fished or played on the bank, and join us gleefully when we left.

We began to wonder if Pal *could* swim. All dogs, we'd heard, swim naturally, and we assumed that Pal could, too, but we'd never actually seen him do it. Try as we would, we couldn't toss him out over his depth. This knotty problem was settled one fall day when we were playing up near the University and came upon an abandoned basement. The cement had been poured, but the house had never been built on top of it. There was about five feet of wall showing, and about three feet of water in the hole, certainly enough to make Pal swim. So, before he realized what was up, we grabbed him and pitched him in. Well, he swam all right, like a drowning rat, but when he came to the concrete wall he naturally couldn't get up. Without a sound he pawed away at the concrete, but there was no way that he could climb up. We reached down and tried to catch him by the scruff of the neck, but couldn't quite make it. We urged him towards the other side where there was a door frame, but he wouldn't go. Finally, there was nothing for it but for me to jump in and heave him out. We never threw Pal into the water again.

Pal's greatest nuisance value, however, was the way he loved to fight. He couldn't fight worth a hoot, being small and light and not too sharp of tooth, but as soon as he saw another dog he would fly at it, teeth bared, and try to devour it. None of your walking about stiff-legged with hackles raised the way most dogs do, and then backing off gracefully, muttering threats and imprecations. No, Pal got right into it, secure in the knowledge that we'd come to his rescue.

He had regular enemies, too. Dogs that he encountered on the routes he took when he was supposedly following us. If we went along Tenth Street, for instance, from MacPherson Avenue, where we lived during his stay with us, towards Broadway, Pal went through all the backyards, chasing cats, ravishing flower-beds, and fighting with dogs. We could always *hear* him – and the hissing, squalling, barking, and swearing that he left in his wake – but rarely did we ever *see* him.

That is, we didn't see him until we met the bread-man. I don't know what company this bread-man drove for, or anything else about him except that he had a big white horse pulling his wagon and underneath it, skulking along, were his two dogs, a Chesapeake and an Airedale.

These two breeds were very common in Saskatoon in the Twenties, although I haven't seen one in years. The Chesapeake is big and short-haired, brown in colour, built something like a Labrador retriever, only stockier. The Airedale is leaner, with short bristly hair and a square muzzle. He looks like a big version of the wire-haired terrier. Both breeds are heavy, muscular and fierce.

It's difficult to believe, when I think back on it, that Pal would attack both of these dogs at once. But he did. Every time he met them. He hated those two brutes as no dog has ever hated anything. He could tell, blocks away, when they were approaching, and would instantly begin to run around in circles, his hackles rising. If we didn't catch him then and hang onto him, it would be too late. He'd be into it with both of them, and we'd be trying to save his hide.

Sometimes we'd grab the dogs by the tails and drag them away from him (not easy with an Airedale), sometimes we'd pelt them with gravel from the road. Always we'd shout and wave our arms and threaten and try to get hold of Pal. And frequently, when we finally got them separated and were leaving the scene, he'd break away, double back and go at it again. Every walk to Broadway was a nightmare.

It wasn't, however, anything like the nightmare at the high school field day in the fall of 1926.

Nutana Collegiate Institute, a majestic high school on the corner of Victoria Avenue and Eleventh Street, at the top of the "short hill", was already an institution with tradition when I entered it that autumn. It was a huge brick building overlooking the river, with an enormous, flat campus, six tennis courts, and a football field. I liked the tennis best. You could play it whenever you liked, so long as you could find one other person to play with. Since I had gone to work for the Saskatoon *Star Phoenix* as a paperboy that same fall, I didn't have an opportunity to play games after school. So I played tennis early in the mornings.

We newcomers had just got comfortably settled into our seats, and were trying to get used to Algebra and French and Latin, when one day the drill and hygiene teacher announced that in a couple of weeks the school would hold its annual track meet. He gave us a pep talk. "It doesn't matter whether you win or not, it's trying that counts. You Grade Nines don't know what you can do best. You've got to try to find out. So get behind this thing and enter."

He was painfully sincere, with a square jaw and piercing eyes. So inspired was I that I went around to his office and entered my name in every junior event. Everything: high jump, pole vault, dashes, long runs, broad jumps of all kinds. The works. The fact that I couldn't do any of these things made no difference. Hadn't he said that it was the trying that counted?

The morning of the track and field meet I was out there bright and early in my baggy gym trunks, prancing about, limbering up with the best of them. I had no notion of what I was doing. Because of my paper route I hadn't trained myself for one single event. Furthermore, there was absolutely no indication from anything I'd ever done in the past that I could even beat an arthritic octogenarian. But still, there I was, brash and self-confident as the keenest-honed athlete, ready, aye, ready for the fray.

The junior events were run off in the morning, to make way for the more dramatic senior programme in the afternoon. The first event was the hundred-yard dash, for which the grounds people had marked off the course in lanes, made by cords strung on little wire stakes. I lined up with the others. Went into a starting crouch as I saw my neighbour do. Quivered with expectation, waiting for the starting gun to go off. And when it did, sprawled flat on my face.

This saved me from being last (it was, in fact, the only race in which I didn't occupy that position). The two-twenty-yard dash was next, I remember, and this time I got under way all right without falling down. I actually managed to get all the way around the track. I wasn't lapped by the front runners, either, but that may have been because the race was only once around the track. And neither was I actually last. There was one other runner behind me. My dog.

Pal had followed me to school this morning, and was taking a real interest in the proceedings. There were no other dogs around to fight with, so he contented himself with trotting languorously across the track in front of the crouching runners, just before the starter pulled the trigger. "Who owns that white dog?" I kept hearing the drill teacher yell, but I was not about to admit that he belonged to me.

It was to soon become painfully obvious, however. Pal decided that if ever a feller needed a friend it was me in those races. And so he trotted around behind me in the four-forty and the half-mile and the mile, in each of which I would have been last except for him. He stayed well back, loping along in his usual hang-tail manner, and after the winners had been applauded and some people politely stayed to watch the last runner come in, there was always a ripple of laughter as he followed me to the finish line.

My sister Phyllis, who was three years ahead of me in high school and thus had a position to maintain, was furious. "Mother!" she complained bitterly at lunch time, "tell Max not to go in any more of those races. He's just making a fool of himself. And that stupid dog, ambling along behind him! I'm ashamed to admit he's my brother."

"Then why do it?" I yelled, my pride seriously bruised.

"I can't help it. Some of them already know you are my brother. Tell him to stop, Mother."

Mother mildly suggested that, since I had about three miles to walk after school delivering papers, it might be a good idea if I saved some of my energies for that.

But I was adamant. I'd entered in all the events and I was no quitter. I ate hardly any lunch, not wanting to add to my weight before the high jump, which came next.

For this event some of the school reprobates – the kind who smoked and swore and even went out with girls, and had no sense of duty when it came to representing their home room – had taken up positions beside one of the standards. They'd equipped themselves with a certain kind of heavy cloth. When torn quickly, it made a loud ripping noise like a pair of pants giving way. Just as I lifted my front leg to clear the bar, they ripped about a yard of this stuff and I was sure my flimsy gym pants had parted. It's very difficult to clear a bar and land in a pit while keeping your legs close together.

The pole vault, the running broad jump, and the running hop-skip-and-jump were equally disastrous. I finished that long, hot day without a single success.

It was a most humiliating day for me, but a most important one because, in one fell swoop, I learned some fundamental things about myself. I was forced to realize my very definite limitations when it came to track and field. I couldn't run faster than anyone, jump higher or further than anyone, or throw anything further than anyone. So I was now able to write those things off completely. No sweating around race tracks in the early dawn, watching my diet, getting plenty of sleep to keep in training. Instead, I could henceforth concentrate on the things that I *could* do – like acting in skits, for instance, or writing pieces for the school paper, or debating. And I could eat and smoke and drink as much as I felt like. It was a great feeling of release I had at the end of that field day. I was free.

However, although I didn't distinguish myself on that occasion, Pal certainly did. *His* great success came right at the climax of the day. The competition between the five forms had been keen and, as we came to the conclusion of the events, C School and E School were tied for points. The deciding event was to be the final heat of the one-hundred-yard dash. I don't know why this particular event was chosen for the honour, perhaps because it was Mr. Manerlie's favourite. (He believed that this short, dramatic sprint really tested the mettle of a boy. He was a great one for testing mettle.)

I can see the scene as clearly in my mind as though it were happening now. That long, straight course, running along the Eastlake Avenue side of the field. The straight lanes, marked off with their strings. And all the student body, their families and friends lined up on either side of the course, bathed in the rays of the warm September sun.

The athletes crouched in their positions. Manerlie, piercing eyes on fire, stood beside them, his starting pistol raised aloft pointing at the sky. "On your marks, get set . . . ."

And then a terrible thing happened. Unnoticed by anyone, the breadman's rig had come down Eastlake Avenue, the old white horse clip-clopping along contentedly, the

Chesapeake and the Airedale trotting beneath the wagon. They came abreast of the contestants just as they were going into their crouch and Manerlie had begun his starting chant.

It was then that Pal, who'd been ranging about looking for trouble, spied them and challenged them to come out and fight. They came, all right, and the three joined battle in the only open space available–right in front of the crouching athletes on the string-marked course.

Oh it was a wonderful scene, rolling, tearing dogs, screaming girls, cheering boys, fainting matrons. Pandemonium complete. Back and forth across that track the three dogs plunged. And I never had any idea that a drill teacher could be so handy with curse words. As he waded in among those dogs, getting himself entangled in the cords, and went down on top of them waving his arm with the starting pistol in it, the language he used would have done justice to a mule-skinner. "Who owns that blankety-blank dog?" he kept yelling.

I didn't wait for the conclusion of the fight. I suddenly remembered that time was passing, and if I was going to get myself changed and down town in time for my papers, I'd have to leave immediately. As I went, I could hear the sound of snarling dogs, screaming girls and swearing men rising into the autumn sky. And when I got down to the bottom of the short hill and started across the old Traffic Bridge, Pal caught up to me. He was unconcerned about the whole thing, probably wondering what all the fuss was about. Several other dogs, attracted by the noise, had come from blocks away to join in the fray, so I guess he felt his presence was no longer needed.

There is only one more thing to be said about Pal, and it grieves me even now to think of it. One day at noon a couple of years later, when Denny, too, was in high school, we came home together. When we walked in the back door Mother was standing at the stove stirring the soup. She didn't tell us to be sure and clean our feet, or to hang up our coats or anything like that. In fact, she didn't even look at us.

As we went past Mother on the way to the dining room where the rest of the family were sitting silently, she stopped us and said, "You'd better go and look at what's at the side of the house." By the way she said it, we knew something very bad had happened. And when we got there we saw old Pal, lying on his side, very dirty, and very dead. He'd been shot through the chest with a twenty-two calibre rifle. There was no blood, just a small, round hole, but it was enough.

He'd barely made it home, Mother told us later, and it was obvious that he'd been shot not far away. Without saying a word, the two of us carried him to the middle of the back garden, dug a big hole and placed him in it.

Then we set out, still silent, to find his murderer. A Mr. Grady lived behind us, his garden, of which he was inordinantly fond, butting on ours. He hated Pal, we knew, because of the havoc done to his tomatoes, sweet peas, and other garden stuff. We knocked on his door.

"Did you shoot our dog?" Denny asked, when Grady came to the door.

He looked at us, two very serious youths standing on his back stoop. "No," he said, "but I wish I had."

Denny's red hair bristled, and his eyes glinted as they did when I'd pushed teasing him too far and he was about to start throwing things. But you can't throw things at an adult and a neighbour. Denny choked back his rage and muttered, "You can't just go around shooting people's dogs, you know. You'll get into trouble."

Mr. Grady slammed the door, leaving us there on his stoop with our wrath and our sorrow. It was no use, we realized. Nobody would ever admit to the act, and besides, Pal was dead. All that energy and splendid nonsense suddenly gone from the world. Gone forever.

I missed him most of all on the long, lonely, miserable walks when I was covering my paper route. Pal always used to pick me up at the Nutana end of the bridge, and dutifully accompany me up and down the long blocks. There were always dogs to fight, cats to chase, and garbage cans to demolish. For months, as I trudged up and down those streets, I'd hear a noise behind me and turn quickly, for a split second looking for Pal. Then I'd realize that, of course, he wasn't there, and never would be again.

14 *To Tread the Boards*

When I was in Grade Eleven, Bramsby Williams came to our school, and I was never the same again. I don't know who arranged for him to come, or why he was touring the country; I only know that one Friday our English teacher announced, with some pique, that we wouldn't be having the regular lesson but instead would go up to the auditorium to hear a famous English actor.

Great. I didn't have my homework done for that period, and was wondering how I'd talk myself out of a detention slip. So up the broad stairway we went, making the usual cracks, pushing each other, the bolder ones ripping out the odd raucous belch. We sat down on the folding chairs and waited, figuring we were in for a boring time, but anything was better than listening to Miss Ranken on Keats.

Then Bramsby Williams came on stage. He was a rather rotund man, not very tall, with hair cut long the way actors often wear it. Actually, a very ordinary-looking guy. Then, before our very eyes, he changed. Everything, his size, his demeanour, his hands, eyes, even the shape of his nose. He was poor, demented Fagin, pleading with Oliver Twist, "That's right, that's right. That'll help us on. This door first. If I shake and tremble as we pass the gallows, don't you mind, but hurry on. Now, now, now!"

Then he was Bramsby Williams again, but only for a moment before he became another Dickens character. This time it was that detestable sneak, Uriah Heep, cringing, gloating, obsequious, "a very 'umble person". Then he was Wilkins Macawber, Mr. Bumble – one after the other he went into the characterizations, and each time there was absolutely nothing there of Bramsby Williams.

I sat on the edge of that folding chair and my eyes popped. I'd never imagined anyone could do such things. Sure, we had plays at the lit. *The Master Builder,* I remembered, and Sheridan's *Rivals.* And the kids who did the parts were good, too. But this! Never in the movies, or anywhere else, had I seen anything like it.

In a daze, I left that auditorium and finished the afternoon. In a daze, I went and got my papers and delivered them. I was so excited that I could hardly walk. This was it. This was what I would be. The living theatre was the thing for me, boy. Nothing less would do.

It took a long time to get Bramsby Williams out of my mind. In fact I never did, completely.

It would be a mistake, however, to believe that there was no live theatre on the Prairies during the Twenties and before. There was plenty. In the tiny town of Hanley, for instance, where my wife grew up, there is an auditorium of great style and pretence, known as "The Opera House". Here was where the local little theatre put on its awful plays, and where the impoverished travelling companies staged *Uncle Tom's Cabin* (with Little Eva hoisted up to heaven on creaking wires), and *East Lynn,* and *Abie's Irish Rose.* Here's where great British actors, like Sir John Martin Harvey, came. I remember his great play, *The Only Way,* and his intoning of those never-to-be-forgotten lines, "It is a far, far better thing that I do than I have ever done; it is a far, far better rest that I go to, than I have ever known." They make me weep just to write them.

And then there were the tent shows with their Tobys and G-strings and Ingénues and Villains. What was a "toby"? Why, he was a bumbling lout who couldn't talk straight, walk without falling over himself, or keep out of trouble. He could make faces fit to kill, and he wore outlandish clothing and, oh my lord, but he was funny. Mickey Rooney made a fortune playing tobys in the movies, and Peter Kastner and Bob Denver, of *Gilligan's Island,* carry on in the same tradition. And a "G-string" is a toby, only older, and of course everybody knows what an ingénue is and a villain.

The Chautauquas, which came once a year, also put on live plays, along with their lecturers, singers and other entertainers. And when the huge Chautauqua tent went up in town, they were sure of a crowd. Always there was the tall, dignified lecturer with his philosophical pep talk, "Attitudes and Platitudes" or "Highways and Byways", intended to inform and inspire. And a deep basso, a piping tenor, a bosomy soprano. As well as a play with real actors. And maybe a specialty act, involving the "visual arts". It was all tremendously uplifting, and guaranteed not to offend any member of the family.

But best of all was the Empire Theatre in Saskatoon. It doubled as a silent movie house when there were no travelling shows, but when the live players came the place burst into life. The Shakespearean companies always needed extras to stand about, and to make up mob scenes or soldiers or other non-speaking parts. These "spear carriers", as we came to call them, were invariably picked from the high school. And since, by this time, I was about as stage-struck as I could get, I was sometimes hired. It was on one of these occasions that I, and the stage of the Empire Theatre, together knew our most wretched hour.

The play was *Julius Caesar,* and the company was a small, obscure one with no famous actors. A group of us were engaged to play the soldiers for the Battle of Philippi. We were to be dressed in Roman armour, and to come in on cues marked "Enter Brutus and Cassius and soldiers". In another scene, we would "Enter fighting".

This was fine. We had no lines to speak, and were instructed merely to fill in the background. The fighting would be done by real actors in the foreground. All that would be required of us would be to sort of run about and shout and gesticulate. Also, as the assistant director instructed us on the night before the performance, "Be careful not to jab anybody in the ass with those spears!"

I really wish he hadn't said that about not jabbing anybody. Such an admonition tends to have the reverse effect on me. With my vivid imagination, I immediately saw just how terrible it would be if I were to jab an important actor in the rear end. How it would affect the actor, the audience, and quite possibly my future career on the stage.

The day of the performance arrived. As always happened while I was in high school, I was in a terrible rush. I had to finish my paper route, have my dinner, and then get back downtown by seven o'clock. Since we lived on MacPherson Avenue at the time, and that was about a mile from the theatre, it was impossible for me to make it. The only solution to the problem was to skip dinner entirely, and even then it was tight.

Thus it was that I arrived at the Empire Theatre fully fifteen minutes late, and very hungry. I have one of those metabolisms that can't go too long without food. Whereas others may feel a bit peckish when eating is delayed, I become extremely irritable and absent-minded, since the only thing I can really think about is food.

I reported backstage with about a thousand other people, all going in different directions. Since the dressing room facilities at the Empire were limited, even for the actors, there was no place for us to get into our faded costumes and rusty tin helmets except in a back corner. A thin, worried man kept counting us to see if he had enough soldiers for a decent army, and as soon as I arrived he threw the costume at me, hissing that I had only a few minutes to get into it.

"Then line up there at the stage entrance with the others," he said. "Oh–don't forget your spear and shield, and keep quiet until you are on stage. Then do just as they showed you last night."

As quickly as possible, I pulled off my pants and shirt and pulled on the short skirt-thing that they'd given me. Then I tied the sandals on my feet, put the helmet on my head, added a couple of arm bands for good measure, and went and lined up with the others.

The assistant stage manager grabbed me and shoved me into place. Then he did a double-take. "For God sake," he hissed, "who ever saw a Roman soldier wearing long underwear!"

Since it was the dead of winter, and winters are cold in Saskatoon, especially when you have to be outside for a couple of hours each evening, I had on a suit of fleece-lined combinations. The legs came down to my ankles and the sleeves down to my wrists.

"Take that stuff off," he said, shoving me back towards the corner.

"But I can't. I haven't anything on underneath it."

"I don't care about that. Take it off. And for God sake hurry!"

So when I finally stumbled onto the stage, accoutred with spear and shield, I had, along with my hunger and nervousness, yet another serious worry. The skirt I had was short and rather tattered, and when I moved I could feel the breezes swirling about my uncovered crotch. Should I happen to get pushed over on that stage, I felt it might result in a certain amount of exposure.

But it was too late to do anything about it. The alarum

had sounded and we must "enter fighting". It is very difficult, I found, to brandish a spear in one hand, hold a shield in the other, and at the same time prevent a wayward skirt from flapping above the knees. I kept myself low and made up with shouting what I lacked in brandishing, and since I was well at the back, I think I might have got away with it if some damned fool hadn't got his short sword caught in my skirt. In desperation I grabbed at it, and my spear went clanking onto the stage floor. The thing to do, I realized afterwards, would have been to leave it there and just go about shouting and gesticulating. But such was my nervous state that I had somehow got the notion that I must have that spear or perish. So down on my knees I went to look for it.

I managed to get it, too, but just as I was getting back on my feet with the spear held horizontal to the floor, instead of straight up as we'd been instructed, somebody bumped me from behind, and I went sprawling forward. The actor playing the part of Cato was just finishing the speech with the words, "I am the son of Marcus Cato, ho!" when the point of my spear and the curve of his backside made contact. The "ho!" of challenge became an "Ohhhh!" of alarm, and he lay there on the floor writhing with pain. Afterwards they said it was one of the most realistic deaths ever staged in the Empire Theatre.

But my most pleasant memories of the old Empire are associated with the annual visit of the Dumbells. It was the high point of the year for us. We'd talk about it for weeks ahead, read all the advance publicity, endlessly go over the skits of the previous year, and try to anticipate what would come this time. We knew the Plunketts like brothers, Captain Merton, and Morley, and Al, who was the first of the crooners to send the girls to swooning.

The Dumbells we saw in the late Twenties were, of

course, only the remnants of the famous "Original Dumbells", who began as a troupe of soldiers entertaining soldiers. It happened in the blood and muck of the First World War trenches, when Merton Plunkett, a YMCA entertainment organizer, began to gather talented men from the ranks for his small, front-line shows.

As the men came out of the trenches, tired, dirty, and unbelievably war-weary, he would gather them together and stage an impromptu entertainment. They'd sing *It's a Long Way to Tipperary* and other war songs, tell corny jokes about army life, getting as many soldiers as possible into the act. Female impersonation naturally went over big with the soldiers, and somebody was always putting on a wig and doing a dance, or singing a song and displaying a naughty bit of leg. It always brought down the house. Thus did Ross Hamilton transform himself into a tall, beautiful woman with a fine soprano voice.

Gradually, the show took shape, and the best of the entertainers were withdrawn from the trenches to become permanent troupers. They travelled about France staging their show in barns, on the back of a truck–anywhere they could find–often within sound of the guns. As their audiences and fame grew, their show improved, until it was a fast-moving, slick and professional review.

In London on leave, the Dumbells played four weeks at the famous Coliseum, and when they returned to Canada they formed themselves into a professional troupe. And after an eight-week run in the Grand Theatre in Toronto and a good run in New York, they began their Canadian tours, which were to take them many times back and forth across the country.

By the time we saw them, they had picked up some new professional talent, such as the "silly ass" Englishman, Fred Emney, the rubber-legged waif, Pat Rafferty, the suave straight man, Charlie Jeeves, and tenor, Cameron Geddes.

And they still had Ross Hamilton, and another female impersonator, adagio dancer Glen Allen.

And they were funny! Most of their material came from London music-halls. They did all the old "turns"–the classroom bit, the barber-shop bit, the policeman bit, the dope-fiend bit, the telephone bit–and I can still remember most of those turns, almost word for word.

I can remember, too, dashing through my paper route, bolting my supper, and galloping down to the theatre to get in line for the rush seats in the gods. We had to stand outside in the freezing cold, and wait, and wait, and wait. But deep inside us was a warm feeling of anticipation, a bubbling laugh already forming, ready to burst out as soon as Red Newman appeared on the stage.

Then the long climb up the outside stairway to the top balcony; the long wait in the cramped seats of the gallery, talking, whistling, dropping peanuts on the heads of the people below. Finally that great moment. The pit orchestra swung into a medley of war tunes. The house lights went down, and the velvet curtains parted, revealing the asbestos curtain with its advertising signs painted on it; then that too went up to reveal the stage.

And there, at last, was what we'd been waiting one whole year to see. That stage, and those people, singing, clowning, dancing. The show was fast and clean. While an elaborate set was being put in place behind the curtain, Red Newman would be out front in his wild red wig and unbelievably sloppy uniform, his puttees dangling, singing *Oh It's a Lovely War*, in his gravelly Cockney voice. "Up to yer knees in wortah, up to your waist in sluuuush!" and on and on–"Ain't a shaiym to tike the pie, Who wouldn't be a sojer, aih?" It was a great song by a great artist, and it took every soldier in the house right back to the days when he was up to his own waist in slush and misery.

Then, for the ladies, it was Al Plunkett. Long before

Rudy Vallee titillated the girlies with his falsetto crooning, even longer before Sinatra had the girls screaming, slight, dapper Al Plunkett was winking at them slyly and singing "No wonder the waves are wild, It makes mother ocean blue – The bathing suits they get disappear when they get wet. . . ." Sophistication. There it was, boy, right in front of us. Suave, smooth, cool. That was Al Plunkett. What a hit he'd have been on television!

But what we really came to see were the skits, featuring Fred Emney, Charlie Jeeves, Red Newman, Pat Rafferty, and anybody else from the cast that might be needed. These were in the best English music-hall tradition. Fred Emney was, I swear, the funniest Englishman I've ever seen. He walked funny, talked funny, made funny faces, and he did it all with a marvellous economy of words and movement. A shrug, a raised eyebrow, a grunt (in an English accent) could bring forth a spontaneous roar from the audience.

Newman and Rafferty were more obvious, more frantic, louder and wilder. They worked hard for their laughs, fell down a lot, smashed things, shouted, fought – but they, too, were marvellously funny. Rafferty played the poor little put-upon tramp, a sort of Stan Laurel to Newman's Oliver Hardy. He dressed in baggy, tattered clothing, and used a dead-white make-up. When being bawled out by Newman, he could shiver and shake until you'd swear he was going to fly apart.

Ross Hamilton always came out in a beautiful gown and big hat, and sang soprano. Imagine it. A real female impersonator. But they were very big in the Twenties, and people took them seriously. The house rocked with applause after his sentimental song, *Danny Boy* or some similar tune, not so much for the quality of the singing as for the fact that he was doing it. "Imagine that, eh? You'd never *know* he was really a man." Thinking back on it now, I can't for the life of me figure what was so all-fired wonderful about a man pretending to be a woman, but such are the vagaries of taste in entertainment.

Glen Allen, a small, lithe man in a blond wig and appropriate padding, did an adagio dance with a male partner. He was very good, too, and we all applauded mightily.

Those were the more innocent–or perhaps the more short-sighted days. Words like "homosexual" and "transvestite" weren't kicked around as freely as they are now. Dressing up like a woman, and singing and dancing like one, was looked upon as a damned clever trick–something like sawing a female in half, or making a rabbit disappear–nothing more.

At the beginning of the second act, the scene was familiar to us all, and standard with the Dumbells. The stage was fitted out like a drawing-room, with comfortable chairs and a grand piano. Most of the cast were on stage, immaculate in evening dress, as though to reassure us that although they clowned around a lot, they were really sophisticates at heart.

We loved this. Most of us had never seen anybody in a tuxedo before. Then Captain Plunkett would get up and make a little speech about how nice it was to be back in Saskatoon, and introduce his fellow cast-members. Then he'd say something like, "Now, Harry, if I accompany you, will you sing one of those lovely Irish ballads?" And Harry Binns would nod, butt out his cigarette and saunter over to the piano, where the Captain was already seated, drop one hand lightly on the lid and sing *Mother Machree*. He had a high Irish tenor, such as you rarely hear any more, and the Empire Theatre rang with the golden tones of it.

Then it would be Cameron Geddes' turn, and he'd sing *Asleep in the Deep*, and we'd all marvel at how he could hit those real low notes the way he did. Talk about Paul Robeson!–those of us who saw the Dumbells in the late

Twenties know perfectly well that Cameron Geddes was the finest basso in the world. There he was in the flesh, not on record or on a screen, but *there,* straining and perspiring to do his very best. And every one of us pulling for him every note of the way. Ah, Cameron Geddes, how many sore throats you've given me as I, myself, strained and puffed to get my voice down that low. You were the greatest!

After the final reprise with the entire cast, and after the curtain had come down for the final time, we'd find our way out of the theatre in a daze. Out into the frosty briskness of Twentieth Street, to walk up Third Avenue and across the bridge, talking, talking, talking about the show. Laughing again at the antics of Rafferty and Newman, marvelling anew at the skill of Emney, saying the lines over and over, and still laughing ourselves silly. We'd indulge in this same re-hashing as the long winter wore on, and the greatness of the show would grow with the repeating.

We'd do more. Some of us, as I have said, were stage-struck. Dennis Hamer and I would steal the material from the Dumbells, add a few local touches and maybe even originate a joke or two, to make skits of our own which were put on at the high school "lits". Just about anything went at the lit: singing, reciting, and acting. Often, the kids from the Ukrainian Institute dressed up in their national costumes and performed their native dances. The lits were a great outlet for local talent.

Since neither Dennis nor I wanted to always be the straight man and let the other have all the jokes, we would alternate. In one skit he'd be the comic and I the straight man. In the next, we would reverse the order. Dennis, who was English, looked very funny in plus-fours and a monocle, and could read a comic line. He was, however, inclined to become over-enthusiastic and frantic when we weren't getting the laughs we expected. On one such occasion, during the barber-shop skit (one of our best) when we ended up eating the shaving cream (whipped cream, really), the audience sat stoney-faced and silent instead of rolling in the aisles. Dennis completely lost his cool. His antics with that whipped cream became crazier and crazier, until finally he dumped the whole dish of it over my head. The white sheet I had on covered only my shoulders, so that most of my only good suit was covered with the sweet, sticky mess. There was nothing in the family budget to provide for dry-cleaning.

I don't know where the members of the Dumbells are today. Many of them have passed on to that greater stage in the sky, while others, I'm sure, live in peaceful retirement, dreaming of those days when they made Canada laugh. Everybody, I suppose, has his nomination for the most important man who ever lived. To me the best of the lot was that bouncy, shrewd, resourceful Captain Merton Plunkett, who got the Dumbells together and gave a generation of prairie-bound sodbusters a notion of what show business was all about. He doesn't even rate a listing in the *Encyclopedia Canadiana,* but to me he is still the greatest.

In later years, after I'd left the dry, wide prairies and become a journalist of sorts, I wrote an article for *Maclean's* magazine called "The Rise and Fall of the Dumbells". My research took me to Collingwood, and to the home of Captain Plunkett. I was as nervous and excited as I'd have been meeting the Queen herself. Me, actually talking to Captain Plunkett! I had, indeed, arrived.

15 *To Increase in Wisdom and Stature*

Boys' Parliament, that national organization which gave to those qualified an early insight into the political ways of grown men, was an important part of many a teen-ager's life. In my own case, I never would have made it if a kid hadn't got hit on the side of the head with a hockey puck.

My family had always gone to Grace United Church, which was on Tenth Street, two blocks away from Westminster Church, which was on Twelfth Street, and I had gone to Sunday School there, too, until the year I went into Nutana Collegiate.

As I have already said, I, like most prairie kids, had a passion for hockey. And one evening I was down at the open-air rink on Broadway, playing sub for the Grace Church Midgets, or Sprouts, or whatever the little kids were called. I wasn't getting much ice-time because, as I've pointed out, I was neither very quick nor very aggressive, two extremely necessary attributes in a hockey player. Well, our goalie got hit in the face with a puck and quit. One of the other players looked at me and said, "Hey, why don't you go in goal? You'll get more ice-time than anybody." So I did.

I buckled on the big heavy leg pads and the belly pad and took the goal stick and went and stood in goal. And now a funny thing happened. If you've ever watched kids play hockey, you'll notice that when the forwards get a chance to shoot at the goal they invariably shoot at the goalie. If he can't move fast enough to get out of the way, the puck hits him and he makes a save.

Well, since I couldn't move fast, the first puck that was shot at me hit me on the leg pad and bounced away. Everybody shouted, "Good save!" This went on and on. Once a forward got right through the defence on what is known as a "breakaway". It was just the two of us then. As he came towards me, I coasted towards him and sprawled all over the ice–another thing that I did rather well. The puck hit me somewhere and bounced away and everybody once again yelled, "Great save!" I was the goalkeeper.

Then I discovered another thing. Nobody really wants to be goalkeeper. For one thing, there is always the danger of being hit in the face or some other unprotected part of your anatomy. Also, you have to stand still and, since all of our games were played on open-air rinks and the temperature was often 30 below zero, you get mighty cold. And you also have to carry these big pads to and from the game, instead of the lighter equipment of the other players.

So, in our next game I was once more stuck with being in goal. And I once more made some great saves. I even caught one puck. I was pretty good at baseball (catcher, naturally) and when I saw this high puck coming my way I dropped my goal stick and caught it with both hands. A little unorthodox, but effective. Once again everybody yelled, "Great save!" It was heady stuff and I was hooked.

At this point I must introduce Peggy O'Neil. His real name was James O'Neil, but with that last name the nickname of "Peggy" was inevitable. He was a smallish, tough Irish kid and the best hockey player I've ever known. Long after I knew him, he went on to star for the Saskatoon Junior team, and then to play with the Boston Bruins in the National Hockey League.

Back in 1926, he really couldn't skate very well, but he could stick-handle like a fiend. He was always where the puck was. After any scramble he usually came up with it, and he was able to move his stick with such quickness and dexterity that it was almost impossible to get it away from him. To be sure, he'd rarely pass the puck to a team-mate, any more than he'd relinquish it to an opponent, but in those days of no forward pass or blue lines, the ability to keep the puck was far more important than good combination. And Peggy sure could keep that puck.

When Peggy wasn't playing, he hung around the rink watching other games. So he witnessed my début as a goalkeeper. Right there and then he began to work on me, and he was just as cunning and persistent off the ice as on it.

"Why don't you come to Westminster Church Sunday School?" he asked.

"Why should I?"

"Well, we've got a great class. Meet Sunday morning instead of in the afternoon with the rest of the Sunday School. Do just about what we like. And Napoleon Yake is our teacher."

Mr. Yake was one of our English teachers at Nutana, and I liked him.

"He lets us do anything we want," Peggy went on. "We don't have any of that religious stuff. Talk hockey most of the time, and we're going to have the best midget team in the city. We need a goalkeeper."

"But I'm no good," I countered modestly, hoping he would protest.

"That doesn't matter. Hell, we'll see to it nobody ever gets a decent shot at you. Besides . . ." a belated afterthought, "I've seen you make some saves."

And so it was that I switched Sunday Schools. Mother put up a token protest but, after all, I was going to Sunday School voluntarily, and that was more than any of her other boys had ever done. Every Sunday morning we met in a small room in the basement of Westminster Church, about eight of us, and talked hockey. Mr. Yake was a small, compact, courtly man with no children of his own. He loved hockey, and I'm sure he loved every one of us, especially Peggy O'Neil.

We played hockey and won the championship of the city for our division that year, and the next year, and the next year and the next. From standing in goal and having pucks peppered at me, I gradually learned a little bit about how to stop them and, although I got hit in the head a few times, miraculously I had no teeth knocked out. Which is more than could be said for the others. My recollections of those years were twofold–freezing my feet and watching players spit bloody teeth out onto the ice, and, just as often as not, keep right on playing.

Boys' Parliament? Oh yes. The officials of the Sunday School decided that since the boys of Mr. Yake's class actually liked to go to Sunday School, maybe the same idea would work for all the boys of the church. So they organized the Westminster Boys' Club, which met at ten in the mornings and was run along more or less democratic lines. We had a president and all the other officers, elected by the boys themselves.

In 1929, the Tuxis Boys' Program, originated in 1914 by E. Taylor Statten, was going strong, and great rivalry developed between the different boys' clubs in Saskatoon as to who would represent them at the Boys' Parliament to be held in Regina. Two parties were organized, since you can't have a decent election without developing some rivalry and competition and mud-slinging. They were called the "Four-Square Party" ("square" hadn't yet acquired its opprobrious connotation) and the "All-Round Party". I was somehow selected as a candidate for the All-Rounders and, in company with others, I went about on Sunday mornings visiting other Sunday School classes to make speeches and gain votes.

And then a strange thing happened. Although I was a conscientious enough boys'-clubber, I was also a writer of, and actor in, skits, and I simply couldn't take this thing of the election seriously. So while my opponents gave talks that were terribly earnest and sincere and dull, using a lot of phrases about "healthy minds in healthy bodies", and "youth of today is on the march", and "the future of our country is in our hands", I just couldn't do it. I'd try. I'd think of some great phrases to spout, but on the way from my brain to my mouth something would happen to them, and they'd come out funny. The more serious and profound I attempted to be, the more that little devil would get in there and knock it just enough off balance to be ridiculous.

The first time this happened I was as surprised as the audience. I was the fourth boy to speak, and the strain of trying to be serious and sincere was visibly telling on our listeners. Their faces were strained and pinched with purposefulness. I stood up, also trying to look purposeful but succeeding only in looking silly, and started off to say: "Fellow Tuxis Boys, I've come here to show you that I am serious about my intentions. . . ." Unfortunately, the little demon got in there and it came out: "Fellow Tuxis Boys, I've come here to snow you . . . ." The aptness of this slip so appealed to me that I couldn't help but follow it up. And what an audience! The release was so great that they howled at every remark I made. The same thing happened at every other meeting. I got elected easily.

Certain things stick in my memory about that week at Boys' Parliament. Eating grapefruit for the first time; the Regina tornado; hearing Jimmy Gardiner speak, and the unbelievable pomposity of it all.

It is customary to talk today about the superiority of the youth of the Twenties to the hippies, teen-agers, and flower children of the Sixties. Bull feathers! The big difference was that then we respected the Establishment, believed in it, swallowed all its platitudes and, most of all, planned and schemed and plotted to get into it. Today's young people are hep. They don't swallow all they are told. They see there are some terrible inconsistencies and hypocrisies and injustices in the Establishment and they want to basically improve things. We took what we got; they reject it. Certainly theirs is the healthier, more exciting, more meaningful attitude.

The principal debate at the Parliament was–what else? –whether boys should smoke or not. And in the midst of it all one silly ass got up and pronounced obsequiously that "if the Creator had meant us to smoke, he'd have put chimneys in our heads." That was the first time I'd ever heard that pooferish, completely irrelevant remark, but not the last. I'm sure that in every year, right up to and including this one, I've been the innocent witness of somebody getting to his feet, pursing his lips, and saying exactly the same words in exactly the same asinine way. So much for the campaign against smoking.

Each member of the Boys' Parliament was billeted with a Regina family. I was lucky enough to draw an elderly doctor, who had a beautiful home and a gracious wife. It was a completely new experience for me. A room of my own, a bed of my own–the first time I'd ever slept without at least one other body in bed with me–and grapefruit for breakfast!

Dr. Holmes had been living in Regina on that awful June day in 1912, when the tornado roared through the city, sweeping most of the water out of Wascana Lake, demolishing the Methodist Church and the Baptist Church, lifting houses off their foundations as though they were toys, killing twenty-eight people, and injuring hundreds more.

"The worst of it was," Dr. Holmes explained, "that there was a lot of construction going on then, and the wind picked up the sand and blew it into the cuts of the wounded. We had an awful time cleaning up those wounds."

We also went to a huge banquet in the Saskatchewan Hotel, the first time I'd ever been in a big hotel, and it was great. Five courses. Waiters and waitresses sliding around, looking after you as though you were the King of Siam. Everybody saying nice things. And then the Honourable James G. Gardiner, premier of the province, speaking to us. What a speaker! He just opened his mouth and let it pour forth, scarcely ever pausing for breath. He beat you down with words. I sat there in awe. How could it be that a man could do so much just with his voice? Many times after that I heard Jimmy Gardiner speak and he always had the same effect on me.

After Boys' Parliament was over, one of the Boys' Club leaders asked me to take over a Trail Ranger group and I agreed. My trouble was that I agreed to things much too easily. I needed a Trail Ranger group like I needed a half-ton weight on my back. Besides my junior matric classes (and they were tough, no spares at all), I worked after school and on Saturdays as a boys' sales organizer for the *Pictorial Review* magazine, I played hockey about twice a week, and I wrote and acted in skits whenever I could get the chance. It's easy to see why I got into very little devilment; I didn't have the time.

But oh, that Trail Ranger group! I wake up screaming when I dream of it. Teaching kids in Sunday School or having them in groups is hell on earth. You have all the annoyance and worry of a school teacher, but no power to exert discipline. The kids obey you or don't, as the whim takes them. They play tricks on you, badger you, con you and abuse you in any way their nasty little minds can devise.

Besides this, I had absolutely no talent for Trail Ranger teaching. I'd been an indifferent member of the Wesley

Church group in Prince Albert, and had failed to win one single badge. I'd been too busy playing tricks, badgering, conning and abusing my leader. Such is poetic justice.

Two things stand out amidst all the other horrors of that summer. One of them happened on a pleasant June evening when I arrived home at about 8 o'clock. I'd taken a group of my reluctant magazine salesmen out on a "mop up". That is, there were some magazines left over at the end of the month and they had to be sold. This was "hard sell" in earnest. Instead of sending the kids out on their own, I'd pick out five or six of my best boys and go with them. Up and down the streets we'd go, calling at every house, until the last magazine had been sold. It was foot-wearying, nerve-wracking work.

When I finally arrived home tired, hungry, sweaty and mad, I was alarmed to see a dozen kids sitting on our front lawn, each clutching a small bundle of wieners or marshmallows. "Hi, Max," they shouted. "You promised to take us on a hike tonight! We waited at the church but you didn't come. Can we go now?" What could I do? The river bank was only a block away and, after all, one can't break one's word to kids.

My second frightful memory is as follows. Because of my work, I was often late arriving at the church hall Thursday evenings. The kids were always there ahead of me, putting in their time at breaking chairs, writing on the walls, jumping over tables. One cold winter night I opened the door to have my nostrils attacked by the foulest smell on earth. I couldn't figure it. So acrid, so pungent, so terrible. There was something about it faintly familiar, but it escaped me. It filled the church hall then, and for many days and weeks to come. In fact, I wouldn't be surprised to find it still lingers nostalgically in the corners and under the platform.

"What in the world is that?" I asked as soon as I got in.

The group were all seated in a circle, quiet and attentive, a sure indication that something very wicked had been perpetrated. Nobody spoke.

"Well, what is it?" I repeated. And then, for some reason, I added, "It smells as though somebody wet down the hot air register!"

That did it. Faces that had been getting redder and redder through keeping such a delicious secret burst forth in mirth. I couldn't help but join them. The humour of the situation grew so strongly on me that I completely lost control of myself. I howled with laughter. I clutched my sides and moaned with glee. I rolled on the floor helpless with giggling.

The next Sunday morning the smell was still strong upon our meeting hall, and the place was packed with grinning boys. It was a record turnout. Ninety-eight-point-four per cent against the previous high of seventy-two-point-nine. The word had circulated through the kid grapevine, and nobody wanted to miss the fun. The superintendent never batted an eye throughout the whole proceedings, which he cut a little short, and afterwards he told me that maybe with all my other duties perhaps I should give up the Trail Ranger group. I agreed.

16 *The Man to Hire*

The best thing that happened to me when I was seventeen was that I went harvesting. And the best thing about *that* was that I got to know my brother Morley.

Morley was rarely home. Oh, in Prince Albert I remember him being with us for a while in the winter, but he got back to Nokomis as soon as he could to work on a farm. In Saskatoon, he occasionally showed up in the winter and drove a delivery rig for the Hudson's Bay Company department store, but he'd be gone again come seeding time.

Whenever I think of a prairie wheat farmer I think of Morley, for he was as good a prototype as you'll ever find. Religious, practical, and straight-forward, with a loud, resonant laugh, he loved to tell stories, he loved horses, and he loved the land. Everything about farming was a joy to Morley, even milking cows. Long after he stopped raising his own food he still kept a cow–just for the fun of milking her.

Aside from all this, Morley could fart better than any man I ever knew. All the Braithwaite boys were good farters, but Morley was the best. "A farting horse will never tire; a farting man is the man to hire," he would say, and he believed it. It was his boast, and he wasn't given to idle boasts, that he once stopped a six-horse team by farting at them.

I don't know the anatomical explanation for farting, but I know that it can't possibly do any harm to the practitioner's health. His social standing perhaps, his love life maybe, but not his health. It can, however, contribute tremendously to sibling discord. I remember one winter in Saskatoon when Hub was working at Bob Gordon's fruit store and eating as much fruit as he could hold. All night he released the vilest farts of all time. I was sleeping with him, and I know.

He was playful about it, too. "Heads under cover place!" he would shout, after releasing a putrilaginous sneaker, and then he would yank the covers up over both our heads. Whereupon I would let out a pitiful scream, "Ma–Hub's making smells again!"

After which I'd leap out of bed, pull all the covers off, shake them violently, and throw open the window to the thirty-below-zero cold. It didn't do any good. The vileness of those fruit-farts would seep up through the folds of the covers all night long, and haunt my every dream.

But back to Morley and farming. As soon as a Braithwaite boy was ready for the harvesting, Morley was waiting on a farm somewhere in the Nokomis area to give us our ordeal by pitchfork. First, there was a couple of weeks of stooking, followed by pitching bundles. You earned the fabulous sum of four dollars a day, and board, and you came home hard as nails, and full of wild tales about the things you'd done and the people you'd met.

It was a sort of coming-of-age thing, like puberty rites among the Watusi, or a belated bar-mitzva. After going harvesting you were a man. Hub went, and was reported to be "better than most grown men" in the harvest field.

So, late in August, I packed my belongings into a cardboard suitcase, and set off for Nokomis. It meant that I would miss at least a month of Grade Twelve, but I was confident I could make up for it. Besides I needed the money so badly for clothing and books that I absolutely had to go, whether I could make up the time or not.

I arrived in Nokomis and looked around fondly. It was the first time that I'd seen it since leaving there twelve years before. It had changed some, but the old stone house was still there. And the school we'd all dashed away from, to see our first aeroplane, looked much the same. The Chinese restaurant hadn't changed much either, but the little building on Main Street, where Dad had his office and where I used to go for nickels, was gone.

It's a peculiar thing. I've been back to the old town many times since that spring day in 1919 when we drove out of it in the Russell and, of course, there have been many changes. But, to this day, the only picture of Nokomis that comes into my mind is the one that was impressed upon it when I was six years old. Whenever I think of the town, that memory, and that alone, is what I see. The back lanes where we played run-sheep-run in the autumn dusk, the vacant lot where we played prisoner's base. The ditch beside the railroad track, called "Shunkies", where we swam nude and showed off for the passenger trains roaring by.

Morley met me at the station with the pick-up truck, and we drove down the dusty road between the fields of ripening grain to the farm of Wick Thompson. It was a good farm. The immense frame house was painted white, and the huge barn a bright red. Numerous well-painted granaries and other out-buildings were scattered about the yard, including a bunkhouse which was to be my home for the next month.

There is a smell in a bunkhouse that is like none other. It's composed of dust, dry straw (the mattresses are stuffed with it), body-odour, horse-manure from the men's boots, horse-sweat, and another smell which I can only describe as the essence of the oh-so-dry prairie in the fall.

There were half a dozen others sleeping in the bunkhouse, mostly transients. The other harvesters, like Cap McLaren and Bowser Jardine, were Nokomis residents who took holidays every autumn from their jobs in town so that they could work in the harvest. They loved it, and they were good. The professionals of the trade, you might say. They could handle a fork with the same skill and dexterity as a painter handles a brush. They never seemed to be working hard, but they got an incredible amount done. And they drove me almost crazy.

"We're going to begin cutting tomorrow morning," Morley informed me. "You'll go with Blooming 'Arry. He's around here somewhere. Probably reading. He's always reading. Anyway, I'll call you in the morning."

He did. At four o'clock.

"Rise and shine. Rise and shine!" he shouted, rattling the wooden door of the bunkhouse. "Time to get up!"

It was pitch-dark and cold. I groped my way into my clothing and out into the frosty, damp morning, down the path towards the house where a pale yellow light was showing. Inside, the house was warm and smelled of frying pork and eggs and hot bread. Breakfast was ready.

Morley was already at the table with a couple of others, while Mrs. Thompson and her daughter, Marion, hurried back and forth from stove to table, fetching plates of eggs and pork and fried potatoes and toast and cups of scalding hot tea.

Hunched over his food, paying no attention to anyone, was Blooming 'Arry. He was an Englishman, and that meant he'd had a rough time on the prairies since his arrival there as a young man, forty years before. For just about the favourite sport of prairie dwellers in the Twenties – and maybe still, for all I know – was Englishman-baiting. They were fair game because they talked funny. They dropped their "h's" or added them onto words where they didn't belong, so that they were usually greeted by some local comedian with "'Ellow 'Arry, 'ave you 'eard of the 'orrible things that are 'appening?" After which, everybody would burst into loud guffaws and slap their knees, while the Englishman would grin good-naturedly, and wonder why that was so funny.

They also had a peculiar way with "a's", and another good laugh was "I hawf to lawf to see the cawf go down the pawth to tyke a bawth on Sunday awfternoon."

I have never been in a small town or on a prairie farm where there wasn't at least one wag who could imitate the resident Englishman to perfection.

Blooming 'Arry – whose name was Harry Bloomington – had long since ceased to be visibly annoyed by this foolish teasing, and had closed more and more into himself. Whatever hopes and schemes he'd had when he first came to this "golden land of opportunity", as the early brochures had described it, had long since been blighted by plain bad luck. Gradually, I pieced together his story. He'd been a gentleman's gentleman in London, and had come to Saskatchewan on a buffalo hunting expedition in 1879, when Saskatchewan was still part of the District of Assiniboine. Seduced by the offer of free land, he left his employer, took up a homestead, and remained to fight it out with wind, drought, early frost, grasshoppers, blizzards, and loneliness. And he had lost.

He'd put up a good fight for a while, though, building himself a sod hut, surviving off the collection and sale of buffalo bones, which he hauled thirty miles to the railway at Lumsden by ox-cart. It was rumoured that he'd once been married to a half-breed girl, and that there were children, but they had all died of smallpox around the turn of the century. Since then, Harry had been a drifter, a hired man, working wherever he happened to be needed, carrying in his little pack all his belongings. And it was one of the items in that pack that enabled me to get closer to Harry than anyone had been in years.

On that first morning, I ate only a little breakfast, since I wasn't very hungry. Besides, it didn't appear appetizing. I'd never had fried potatoes for breakfast before, and the idea didn't seem right somehow–potatoes were for dinner. "Better eat up," Morley warned. "Lunch is a long time away." How right he was!

After breakfast, when a rosy glow was showing in the east, I walked with Harry, our shadows long before us, out into a field behind the barn. Wick Thompson, Cap McLaren and Morley were already in the field cutting the grain with binders. I can still see them following each other down that long, long field, each binder pulled by four horses, cutting the tall, almost ripe grain, binding it into sheaves and dumping the sheaves out in rows as they went. Our job was to follow them on foot and stand the sheaves up in stooks so that they would further ripen and withstand any rain that might come before threshing time.

Harry didn't bother to give me any instruction, but by watching him I soon caught on to how it was done. He walked over to the first sheaf, which was between three and four feet long, picked it up and tucked it under his right arm. Then he picked up another and bounced it up under his left arm. Then he went into a sort of squatting position, jammed the butt end of the sheaves hard into the stubble and leaned the heads together. There they stood as he piled other sheaves around them until he had a little teepee of eight or ten sheaves. Then he moved on to the next pile of sheaves, and built the next stook in line with the first, so as to make a straight row.

It looked ridiculously simple. I picked up a sheaf with my gloved hand, grunted at its weight, got it up under my arm, picked up another and squatted to stand them up.

They fell over. I picked them up again and jammed them harder into the stubble. They fell over again, sliding off each other like a couple of drunk companions. The next time I picked them up by the binder twine that bound them together and it slid off the butt end, spreading the straw about me. It took me about four more tries to get two sheaves to stand up by themselves, and to build a very ragged-looking stook that looked as though it might topple over at any moment. Beside Harry's neat, firm stooks it looked disgraceful.

Then and there I began that part of my education that commences outside of school. Like most high school seniors, I was insufferably arrogant and self-assured. Why an old bum like Blooming 'Arry could never teach *me* anything. Not very likely! What I hadn't realized until then was that Harry was a skilled workman, and I wasn't. Everything he did, he did well, with dexterity and speed. In the harvest field it didn't matter a tinker's damn how much history or literature a man knew; it was how well he could do the job in hand that counted. I was to learn this lesson many times before I went back to Saskatoon.

There was a rhythm to the way Harry worked, I soon discovered. Every move used the amount of energy required for it and no more. He never took an unnecessary step, or moved an arm where it didn't need to go. His squat, gnarled, lean figure functioned like a machine.

And, like a well-oiled machine, Harry never stopped—sheaf after sheaf, stook after stook, row after row down that flat field that stretched endlessly before us. On and on he went. Since we each took the next pile of sheaves available, he never left me behind, but he surely did tire me out. When it seemed that we'd been working about six hours, when my back was aching and I was so hungry that my stomach thought my throat was cut, and the sun was riding so high that I thought it must be just about noon, I ventured to ask Harry the time. He hauled a huge turnip of a watch from the bib pocket of his overalls, peered at it and grunted, "Ten past eight."

"What? I thought you said ten past eight."

"That's what I did say." He held the big watch up for me to see.

"Is it right?"

"Never been wrong in thirty years."

"But it seems so much later. Can't we sit down and have a rest?"

"We don't get paid for sitting."

"But I'm as dry as a board. I've got to have a drink."

"There'll be a jug at the end of the field. Come on, let's get going."

He began again to pick up the sheaves in that precise, neat way that I had come to hate, and stand them up into those perfect stooks. Well no gawd-damned sixty-year-old Englishman was going to make a monkey out of me. So I creaked to my aching feet and went doggedly to work as everything became a blur of bending, lifting, piling. Four hours more of this before lunch. How could I stand it?

Finally we reached the end of the field and Harry stopped long enough to dig down into the deep grass and produce a glass jug, full of yellowish water. He unscrewed the top and handed it to me. I tipped it up and took a long, long pull of the worst-tasting water on earth. The wells of southern Saskatchewan are deep, and the earth is filled with numerous salts. So the water in many places has a sulphury, salty taste which is not improved by sitting in the sun all morning, sparsely sheltered by long dry grass. Just the same, I took a good swig every time we reached the end of the field.

"Better be careful with that," Harry advised. "It's physic."

(I found out what he meant later that afternoon when I could barely get a stook up fast enough to squat down behind it.)

Finally, when I had given up on lunch entirely, I saw a cloud of dust coming towards us over the dry stubble field. It turned out to be the pick-up truck, driven by Marion Thompson. She wheeled up beside us, jumped out and announced, "Lunch time!" Then she produced a huge basket of food and a blanket from the back of the truck, and set them down on the stubble. She looked so nice and fresh and pretty in her skirt and sweater that all my fatigue vanished.

"Hey, a picnic," I quipped. "The fondest thing I am of! You are an angel of mercy. You have saved my life." Then as she got back into the truck, "Aren't you going to eat with us?"

"Nope. This angel of mercy has other men to rescue." With a roar the Model-A pickup bumped off and I was left with Blooming 'Arry and the dry, dry stubble.

Finally the day wore to an end, and the next and the next. For the first week I ached all over, but gradually I began to–as they say on the farm–toughen up. My arm muscles grew hard, and I developed one on each side of my spinal column that felt like broom handles. I even learned to set up stooks that wouldn't fall over, and I gained as much satisfaction from the acquisition of that skill as I have from any other. Harry remained as taciturn as ever, and to mitigate the loneliness and monotony of the long days I developed the habit of talking to him. I told him about our home and the kids I knew and what I thought of them, and I discussed the problem of making up one's mind about the future, and about Mary Patterson, who was currently breaking my heart.

Although he never answered–or perhaps because of it–I opened up to him completely, telling him things that I'd never told anyone. Apart from an occasional grunt or mumble, he said nothing in reply, and I thought he was totally uninterested in my youthful confidences. It wasn't until later that I discovered how wrong I was.

Finally the grain was all cut and stooked, and we were ready for threshing. While the rest of us had been finishing up the last few acres, Wick Thompson and an engineer from town had been working on the tractors and separator so that there'd be no breakdowns during threshing. It's hard for anyone who hasn't experienced it to realize how important time becomes during those fall days. All through spring and summer the farmer had helplessly waited for that wheat to grow, all five hundred acres of it. He'd watched the sky endlessly for signs of rain or hail. He'd poisoned grasshoppers and gophers. He'd stood many a night in late August looking at the clear, star-filled sky, dreading an early frost. The wheat had survived all these hazards, had been cut and stooked, but it wasn't worth a cent until it was threshed.

A drastic change in the weather, a long rainy spell, an early snow, could lower the grade of the grain and cost the farmer all his profit on the entire year's work. Every day that it rained meant hundreds of dollars lost. The sight of a dozen men sitting around on their tails eating their heads off was a nightmare to the farmer. He daren't let the men go during bad weather, because he might not be able to find others. So, every day that was good had to be used to the full.

The crop that year was what Morley described as "fair to middlin' ", which meant that it wasn't any "bumper crop" nor was it a "failure". It would run about twenty to twenty-five bushels to the acre, and since the price that year was about a dollar and a half a bushel there was "an awful lot of money sitting in that field."

The weather remained favourable. The sun shone every day and there was little wind. This is the best time of year on the prairies. The winters are too cold and too windy; the summers are too hot and too windy; the springs are too wet, or too dry, and too windy. But the fall is often gorgeous. The big sun sits in the sky, too low to cause much heat but warm enough for comfort. And at night the great harvest moon comes up and rests on the horizon like a round ball of fire, slowly rising in the clear sky to take its place among the endless stars.

Each night I sat alone in the bunkhouse except for Harry who lay in his bunk reading, so unobtrusive that I forgot he was there, and wrote a letter to Mary, describing the moon, making funnies about the other characters in the harvesting gang, and pouring out my boyish heart. My God – I wrote poetry – I quoted Shakespeare – I was inspired.

But then we started threshing. Threshing! I had thought that I'd seen the ultimate in back-breaking toil while stooking, but compared to threshing it was a game of marbles. There is no work in this world, I'm convinced, as difficult as pitching bundles. I mean, of course, for the beginner. It kills your back, ruins your hands, and fills you with dust and chaff. You're convinced that you'll never be able to walk another step. And along with all that there are the horses.

I don't know why, but there is absolutely no rapport between me and horses. They hate me. The first morning of threshing Morley took me into the steaming interior of the big red barn, walked up beside a nice, gentle horse and showed me how to curry-comb and brush him, and then to put on the bridle and harness.

"After you get your team harnessed, you just run them out of the stall and they'll go to the trough for a drink and wait for you to come and hitch them up." He did it. His horses did it, and I tried the same thing with my two.

Their names were Gent and Lady. Believe me, she was no lady and for that matter he was no gentleman. I walked up into the stall beside him and said, "Whoa, boy, whoa," as I'd heard Morley do, rubbed his nose gently as Morley had done, took the bridle off the peg as Morley had, and tried to put it on. But instead of nuzzling his nose down into it like Morley's horses, this damned fool tossed his head about eighteen feet in the air, where I couldn't possibly reach it. And he wouldn't bring it down. Finally I had to climb up on the manger, leap at his head with the bridle extended and, dangling there, work the bit between his clenched teeth. It took four tries, but I managed it. He was equally unco-operative when I put the collar and harness on him, leaning over against me and crushing me against the side of the stall, just for good measure.

After a half-hour struggle I got both horses harnessed, and turned them out into the barnyard as directed. Did they go to the water trough for a drink, as all the other horses had done, and as they themselves had done every blasted morning of their evil lives? They did not. No sooner had they got outside the barn door than they tossed their heads in the air, dilated their nostrils, whinnied, kicked up their heels and galloped out of the gate into the field. How about that?

"I've never seen that team do a thing like that before," Morley averred when he could stop laughing. "They've caught on that you're a greenhorn. Horses'll sometimes do that to a greenhorn. They can always tell."

He jumped on one of the other horses and rode out after the runaways. They didn't avoid him. They came back calm as lambs, but I noticed that they were watching me from the corners of their mean little eyes, and I could have sworn one winked at the other.

Then came the hitching to the hayrack. This was a simple enough manoeuvre. You snapped one end of the neck-yoke onto each horse's collar, slipped the end of the wagon-tongue through an iron ring on the neck-yoke, hitched the traces to the single-trees, threw the lines up onto the rack, jumped onto it, shouted "Ha", clucked your tongue a few times and the team proceeded in a forward direction, dragging the rack behind them. Nothing to it.

Nothing to it, that is, if one horse will step over the

wagon-tongue to get on the other side of it and if both horses will stand still while you do your thing, and not swivel their rumps away out at an angle so that you can't get the traces hooked. They will do all these things just fine all year round until a greenhorn gets hold of them and then, like mischievous kids, they do everything wrong. Act as though they'd never seen a hayrack before in their misbegotten lives, and had never been hitched to anything.

At last I got Lady and Gent hitched to the rack and was ready to go. Morley had told me, "Just two things to remember: always go through a gate straight on, at right angles to the fence, or the ass-end of the rack will hit the gate post. And don't turn too sharp or you'll break the reach." (The reach is the long pole that "reaches" between the front and rear axles of the wagon.) I wish he'd never mentioned those two things.

I jumped onto the rack and clicked my tongue for the horses to begin. I was a little self-conscious because all the others who were already hitched hadn't driven off but, instead, were waiting for me to go first. I soon discovered why. I'd hitched the horses on the wrong sides so that the reins were reversed. Let me explain. At the end of each rein there are two straps, a long one and a short one. The short one snaps onto the outside of the bit of one horse, while the long one snaps onto the inside of the bit of the other horse. So, when you pull on a line, you are pulling on the same side of each bit. But if you get them reversed, it's the short straps that cross over to the other horse so that when you pull on the reins you pull the horses' heads together. They walk along like a couple of lovers, with heads tight together and rumps V'd out on each side. It looks very funny, and just about kills the old hands who wait around for the greenhorn to do it. I've never heard men laugh so loud.

Well, I finally got the horses reversed and out of that gate into the field, where the neat windrows of stooks stood waiting to be loaded onto the racks and hauled to the separator. Morley showed me how to drive the team along beside the windrow and fork the sheaves into the rack, building the load carefully so that the sheaves wouldn't fall off when it got high.

"Just two things to remember," he cautioned (him and his damned "two things"), "you've got to keep your turn at the feeder. Cap McLaren goes in first, and then Bowser, and then you. Don't get behind or you'll have a hell of a time catching up. The other thing is to pull in good and close to the feeder, so you won't have so far to pitch the sheaves. Okay, you're on your own."

So I began pitching bundles. Very easy, actually. You have this long-handled, three-tined fork. You jab it into the sheaf and pitch it onto the rack. As the load gets higher you jam the sheaves down hard on the side, with their butt ends out and heads in, and keep pitching sheaves into the centre. When you are finished you've got a load that is a good seven feet high, and looks like a square box except that it's rounded at the top. While you are loading, the team, who are used to this work, walk along beside the row of stooks and you don't even have to drive them. Just shout at them.

So I began loading my rack in a good steady pace–one sheaf at a time. Felt kind of good. My muscles were hard from stooking, and I considered that this job wasn't going to be bad at all. I'd just nicely got the bottom of the rack covered when I looked over to see how Cap was getting on. He'd already built half his load. I watched him in awe. Working like a machine, in perfect rhythm, he jabbed his fork into the stook, picked up not one but *three* sheaves at a time, and pitched them onto the load. Right there he was tripling my speed. He had other tricks, unnoticed by me at first, that increased his advantage tenfold. There and then I quit dallying, dug my fork into the stooks and heaved like a madman. And I never slacked that crazy pace.

It availed me little, however. Before I was half loaded I saw Cap perched atop his sheaves jostling his way towards the threshing outfit, which was now ready to start transforming those sheaves into wagon-loads of grain and huge stacks of straw.

The tractor started up, the long, sagging belt between it and the separator began to move, all the wheels of the separator whirred and rattled, the whirling knives of the feeder flashed in the sun. Cap moved his load in beside the feeder, stood up on it, and began tossing sheaves down into its hungry maw. Wisps of straw spouted out of the blower to drift leisurely to the ground, and the threshing had begun.

I was too busy pitching those bundles onto my load to watch it, though. Long before I was loaded I saw Cap driving his empty rack away from the feeder, and Bowser pulling his full one right in behind so that there would be scarcely a pause during the transition. Frantically I redoubled my efforts, and by the time Bowser pulled out I managed to limp up to the outfit with about two-thirds of a load.

Now I had to direct my fickle team up close to the feeder to pitch off my load. A threshing outfit was a noisy, dusty place, redolent with the clangs, squeals, rattles and bangs of hundreds of moving parts. To me it was like running the gauntlet with sure disaster barely inches away. In order to see properly, I had to stand up on the load, precariously balanced on uneven and shifting sheaves. Somehow I made it, and there, four feet below me, was that awful feeder with its revolving canvas floor and its murderous chewing knives. Horrible stories were told of greenhorns who had fallen into a feeder and been mangled by those blades. It was a picture that haunted me.

The expression "separate the men from the boys" is a tired cliché but an apt one when it comes to a threshing gang. That is one place where you become a man, or you don't. You are judged by nothing save your ability to keep your turn, to build a good load, to pull your weight, to work like a man. Nobody to help you or to coddle you along or make allowances. You damned well do it or you don't, and you are forever pegged by the gang as a "good worker" or a "bum". Like most other aspects of life on the plains, threshing is ruthless, tough, and painfully revealing of character.

Not that I was thinking of any such things during my first day of threshing. I was too busy getting my load off, and urging my team back to the stooks for another. And inside me was developing a cold fury – such as invariably comes over me at times when I am feeling particularly inadequate. I would damned well show these hicks, I told myself, that I could pitch bundles better than they could. Of course I never did, but the fury kept me in there pitching. It wouldn't let me quit.

And I was to need all the backbone I could muster before that day was over. I never did catch up. Cap and Bowser and the others were constantly "working themselves into a rest". They'd pull into the threshing machine with a magnificent load while there were still a couple of loads waiting to get into the feeder. Then they'd lie in the sun and doze, or kid around with each other, thoroughly enjoying themselves. But me – I barely managed to get to the feeder as the empty rack ahead of me was pulling away, and then, immediately, I had to begin unloading.

When, at last, the long day ended I was in for one final humiliation from my benighted team of horses. Each of the other men, I noticed, unhitched his team from the rack when the outfit finally closed down, and left his half-filled rack where it stood. Then he simply leapt onto the back of one of his horses and rode the mile back to the barnyard. I tried this, too, but when I climbed onto Gent's back the damned brute bucked me off. Then I tried Lady, and she did the same. The first time I at least managed to hang onto the reins to prevent the team from running away. But the second time I had only one rein, and when I pulled on it the horses began to gallop around me in a wide circle, like circus horses in the centre ring. Round and round they went, with me in the middle hollering madly at them. Faster and faster they sped, until I became dizzy and let go. Then they galloped wildly across the field, trampling the reins to bits.

One half-hour later I dragged myself into the barn to find the team standing in their stalls. They still had to be unharnessed and fed. Outside the barn it was quite dark. I could see the lights of the house where I knew the rest of the gang were already eating, and probably regaling each other with tales of the greenhorn. Further along I could see the dim, unlighted shape of the bunkhouse where I could collapse onto a bed. I was a terrible mess. My feet were swollen and sore. My down-at-the-heel oxfords were no good in the stubble field. My hands had blisters as big as twenty-five cent pieces, and were so swollen I could scarcely make a fist. Finally hunger won out over fatigue, and I staggered to the house, washed up in the shed, and filled myself with roast beef, potatoes, corn, tomatoes, green peas, fresh bread, two kinds of cake, and two pieces of pie. After that I didn't feel quite so sad.

The next day was a little easier, and the next and the next. Gradually I learned enough to be able to function as a bundles-pitcher. I never managed to work myself into a rest as Cap and Bowser did, but I came to realize that it was futile to compete with those experts. They were professionals at their job; I would never be anything but a clumsy amateur.

For two full weeks all went well with Wick Thompson's threshing. The sun shone. The grain poured out of the spout and was hauled off to the elevators. Strawstacks grew on the stubble fields like great golden shaggy beehives. And then the rain came.

There was still about a week's threshing to do, so Thompson couldn't let all of his gang go. Cap and Bowser and Red went back to town, agreeing to return when again the weather was good. Morley had his regular chores to do, and that left old Blooming 'Arry and me alone in the bunkhouse.

There was no reading matter in the bunkhouse, and I envied Harry his private stock. Finally, in desperation, I asked him if he would lend me a book. He looked at me with his watery blue eyes, and then dug into his pack and produced a tattered volume. "Ever read this one?" he asked. "It's my favourite."

I took it from him and glanced at the faded title on the cover, *Three Men in a Boat.*

"No . . . I never have," I said, "but I'd like to."

"Don't know if you'll care for it or not. Kind of old-fashioned."

"That doesn't make any difference."

"About England, too."

"I've read lots of books about England. Hardy is my favourite."

"He is? Well then, you may like this." His attitude suggested a fond dog-owner who is afraid that a stranger may not appreciate his pet. I took the book from him and began to read, conscious of his beady eyes upon me.

Well, anyone who's ever read the book can guess what happened. After about two pages I was giggling, two more and I was roaring, a couple more and I was rolling on the bunkhouse floor holding my sides. When I finally looked up there was old Harry beaming on me with a most beatific smile. "Well now," he said, "you're human after all."

Thus I was introduced to Jerome K. Jerome, who had died just two years before at the age of sixty-eight. I have re-read his great, funny book many times since that first time I discovered it by the dim, yellow light of a coal-oil lamp in Wick Thompson's bunkhouse. And every time it makes me laugh just about as hard as it did then.

Even more important than the pleasure I've derived from that book was the fact that it broke down the generation gap, the culture gap, the skill gap, and all the natural suspicion that had existed between me and Harry. He was to produce many more books from that pack–Proust, Thackery, Thoreau, Butler, and a couple by Eric Linklater, whom I also learned to appreciate. He was full of stories, too, was Blooming 'Arry, had a great sense of humour and a fine feeling for beauty. And through all those years, in God knows how many threshing gangs and work parties, he'd been known only as "a funny old Englishman".

Quoting Proust, he taught me that "happiness is beneficial for the body, but it is grief that develops the powers of the mind."

17 *The End of the World*

During the late Twenties somebody was always predicting that the world would come to an end–any day. Signs and portents were everywhere. One religious group, I remember, were so convinced by their own propaganda that they picked out a definite day for the great event. The members gathered on a hill-top somewhere, and waited for the heavenly chariots to come and carry them away. The event received tremendous publicity, with pictures in the newspapers and accounts on radio, but although the group waited and waited all that day and for most of the following week those chariots never came.

The most impressive warning of doom, however, and one that bothered a lot of people, was a message found on the membrane of an egg laid by a hen in Oregon. I can still see the picture in the paper. There it was, an egg with no hard shell, and clearly printed on the membrane the numbers 1928. What else could it mean but that the world would end that year? For some it surely did, but not for everybody.

No, as a matter of fact, the world–at least, the world that we knew–didn't end until a year later, in the fall of 1929. After that, nothing was ever really the same again.

As for me, I was better off that fall than I had ever been.

When it finally came time to leave the farm and go back to school, Wick Thompson paid me off and, for the first time in my life, I had more than one hundred dollars in my hand. It would buy me a new suit of clothes ($27.50 at Tip Top), a new overcoat (another $27.50), new shoes of the very best ($5.00 at the Hudson's Bay Co. department store), underwear, shirts, ties, and still leave me enough to take a girl out a few times.

Mary Patterson. She sang in the Presbyterian Church choir, and for a short while I became a devout Presbyterian. I can still see her standing so straight in her choir gown, head held high, chest out-thrust, making those beautiful mouths that girls make when they sing. I don't know but what a girl looks prettier singing than she does at any other time. My kids often wonder why I, a monotone with no music in my soul, like to watch the *CBC* program *Hymn Sing* on Sunday afternoons. It's because of those pretty girls and the mouths they make when they sing. My kids don't know it, but that's the sexiest program on the air.

So, the first thing I did when I got home was to get dressed in my new clothes and head for Mary's house. I'd talked to the big harvest moon about Mary, and I'd written letters filled with poems about life and love. "There's something there that's so four-square." Now, at last, I'd see her again. And I'd be wearing my new suit.

Ah, that suit. It was gorgeous. Black, with a narrow pin-stripe. The trousers high and pleated, with a tight waist-band. The kind of waist we used to describe as being a little snug under the arm pits. And those pleats. Three on each side, sharp and keen, and the twenty-four-inch bottoms. *Those* were trousers. And the jacket–wide peak lapels, padded shoulders, double-breasted, fitted waist. There was a double-breasted vest, too, also girdle-tight, with flaps on the pockets. I had to admit I looked something like Humphrey Bogart in that suit. Not much, but something.

The shoes were polished mirror-bright. Pointed toes, and metal clickers on the heels.

My shirt was new, my tie was new, even my underwear and socks were new. Never in my life had I been decked out in so much newness. My hair was plastered to my head with vaseline hair tonic, my mouth was scoured clean of that hated affliction your best friends wouldn't tell you about, and I was positively free from B.O. I tell you I was something. True, my face was still a bit burned and chapped from the prairie wind and sun, but after-shave lotion and talcum hid most of that. The blisters on my hands had healed, and my broken and scarred fingernails I could hide by keeping my hands in my pockets.

When I got fully dressed, powdered, deodorized and greased I looked at myself in the mirror, and I guess I never felt better in my whole life. For the first time I'd approach Mary looking and feeling as I wanted to.

I tucked a two-pound box of chocolates under my arm and strode down the sidewalk, my heels clicking, my mind soaring. My God, I was even whistling.

Mary's mother, with whom I had a reasonably good relationship, seemed appalled to see me.

"Does Mary know you're back from the farm?"

"Well, no. I thought I'd surprise her."

"Oh dear–I wish you hadn't."

"I beg your pardon?"

"Perhaps you should have phoned or something."

"Uh . . . yeah . . . but I thought I'd . . . uh surprise her." There was something about the look on Mrs.Patterson's face, as though she were gazing on a dog that had been run over, that plunked a big lead ball in the middle of my gut. "Where is she?" I asked.

"Well . . . um . . . I don't really know. She left about noon. . . ."

"Do you mind if I wait for her?"

"No, you can sit on the verandah here." She shot another quick peek at the box of chocolates, and hurriedly went back into the house.

Just about then a bug rattled up to the curb. A "bug" – I believe the name still holds – was a car that had been stripped down to the chassis and a new body built on. This one had flashy colours, and signs like "Oh you kid" painted on the side. In the front seat were two happy, laughing, wind-blown young people – one male and one female. The girl was my Mary and the boy was a kid I knew and despised, a sheik named Raymond Marchand. Oh God – anybody but Raymond Marchand!

Raymond leapt from the seat, held his arms out to Mary and she jumped into them. Then he kissed her much too thoroughly and let her down. They came up the walk towards the verandah, hand in hand. But I wasn't there. I'd high-tailed through the front door and out the back, pausing only to whisper to Mrs. Patterson, "Don't tell her I was here!"

So I went home and, in the manner of Stephen Leacock's hero, Peter Pupkin, committed suicide. "Frailty, thy name is woman," I kept muttering over to myself, meanwhile cursing Mary. But it didn't do any good. The hurt was too deep and it was not to go away for many months.

That senior year in high school was a bad one. I had to work like a dog to catch up with the rest of the class; I never would have done it except for the help of Elda Stephenson. Elda liked me, sat across the aisle from me and was an excellent student. She didn't have the softness and cuteness and boop-boop-de-doopness of Mary Patterson, but she was a much better sport. She was the best female skater in the school, and I liked to take her skating at the big arena across the river. There, to the tunes of Strauss waltzes, we'd go around and around the ice, arm in arm. It was great fun.

And I'd take her to the show now and then, down to the Daylight Theatre to see John Gilbert and Greta Garbo, and we'd sit in the dark and hold hands. Afterwards, we'd go to the Palace of Sweets for a banana split. Then home again on the street car.

But mostly Elda helped me with my French and Latin authors. I'd fallen woefully behind with both these subjects, and had no way of catching up. History and Literature and Mathematics were easy enough, but I had no aptitude for languages, and so I was hopeless. Besides, being in an exceptionally upset frame of mind, I did little homework. So, when George Bonney, the Latin teacher, would ask me to read my translation of Virgil or Horace I'd stand up and listen for Elda's strong whisper. She always knew the work, and I would simply repeat it after her. It was the same when dear old Miss Smith asked me to read from *La Petite Chose à L'Ecole*, or whatever French book we happened to be reading. Neither of the teachers caught on–at least I thought they didn't–and my good memory enabled me to retain enough of the stuff to pass the examinations.

I also joined the mouth-organ band. This is an experience almost too embarrassing to relate, but, since I'm determined to tell all, it must be included. There was just one little problem about that mouth-organ band. I couldn't play the damned mouth-organ.

The band was organized by our drill teacher, who was also organizer and moving spirit in the Athletic Club to which I belonged. I liked the Athletic Club fine. Every Thursday night a group of us got together in the gym for exercises and club-swinging and tumbling and boxing and kidding around. The only one of these things I was really any good at–I never did manage even the front roll in tumbling–was boxing. For some reason I loved it. To get the gloves on and bash about with another kid my size was, in fact, my greatest pleasure. I had a sneaky left hand and, since I had a pair of boxing gloves at home and did a lot of practising, I actually became champion of the Athletic Club that year.

We wanted to organize a regular band, with trumpets and saxophones and the rest, but when we looked at the prices of these instruments we decided to settle for a mouth-organ band. So we sent away to the Hohner Company, and got great long mouth-organs with four different keys on each – A, C, D and G – really four mouth-organs in one. We had uniforms, too, consisting of white pants and blue blazers.

It's a little difficult for me, thinking back on it, to understand why I became a member of the band when I couldn't play the instrument. The only explanation I can give is that I still hadn't really sorted out this matter of the *differences* between people. I still assumed that, until it was proved otherwise, I could do anything anybody else could do. God knows, it had been dramatically and painfully demonstrated to me that I couldn't run as fast as anybody else, or jump as high, or as far. But I guess I was hard to convince. Anyway, this peculiar attitude was to lead to yet another embarrassing moment.

About those white pants and dark blazer, that was humiliating, too. I had a dark suit coat, which was fine, but the white flannel slacks were a luxury I couldn't afford. So I borrowed a pair from a boy called Ron McGinty – hereinafter referred to as "McGint". The problem with these pants of McGint's was that I didn't return them. I don't know why, I really don't. They hung around the house long after the mouth-organ band had disbanded, and they used to bug me. I'd think of them and say to myself, "I must return McGint's pants." And then I wouldn't do it. Of course, the longer I procrastinated the worse it got, and the more it bugged me. I never took them back.

McGint's pants still bother me. Somehow they've come

to represent all those things I've left undone that I ought to have done. They've become a family legend, too. Anything that is borrowed and not returned immediately becomes a "McGint's pants" in our house.

But even worse was my inability to play the mouth-organ. I think I convinced myself that I could, really. I used to stand beside the piano while Doris banged out *Marching Through Georgia* or *Dem Golden Slippers*–two of our standards–and blow away to beat hell. She'd look very pained at times, but then she'd just bang harder and set her mouth more grimly and say nothing. During band practices the leader would look pained, too, and once he said, "I want each of you to play a few bars alone." When it came my turn I blew something and then *all* the other members of the band looked pained. I don't know why they didn't turf me out right then, but I was president of the Athletic Club that year, and I guess they thought it wouldn't be nice.

Well, we played here and there, and developed quite a repertoire–at least the others did–and we cut quite a figure in our dark blazers and white flannel pants.

Then came disaster. We were playing for the Boys' Banquet. This was the big whing-ding of the year. All the boys in the school had this enormous feed, and there were toasts and speeches and funny skits. It was a great tradition of the school, and each year it was followed by a snakewalk downtown. We all marched along, each with a hand on the shoulder of the boy in front, and wound our way down Second Avenue, in and out of the movie houses and–since it was always held on a Saturday evening–through the Eaton's store, and the Hudson's Bay Company store, and McGowan's Department store. It was a big affair.

As I say, our band was playing at the banquet. I got rather carried away. Usually I just blew gently on the mouth-organ, so that I wouldn't be heard over the others.

(It must have been hell for the other musical kids, hearing this sort of whisper of off-keyness in the background all the time.) But we were marching lustily along through Georgia and since this was my favourite piece I was blowing harder than usual. Suddenly, as by some pre-arranged signal, all the others stopped and I was blowing alone.

Chaos? Not at all. Like the damned show-off I was, I hammed it up–grinned, slid the mouth-organ back and forth across my lips at a great speed, ended with a loud blast and stood up and took a bow. The audience roared and clapped, thinking it was a gag. (At least I felt I had contributed something to the group.) Shortly after that our leader gave up the unequal struggle, and suggested that we go into tumbling exhibitions instead of band work. He knew he was safe from me there.

Years later I came across that four-way mouth-organ in a box of junk. I tentatively placed it to my lips and blew–still hoping for the miracle, but still no music came.

Apart from these activities, the senior high school year was dull, dull, dull. Students today complain about their curriculums being immaterial, irrelevant and obnoxious, but ours was far worse. We complained, too. I can remember one of our brighter students asking the mathematics teacher what possible purpose could be served by learning the binomial theorem. He replied, facetiously, that if nothing else you could dazzle a policeman on the street by reciting it to him. This brought a snigger of appreciation from the rest of us clods, but the boy who asked it was of sterner stuff.

He happened to be the editor of the *Salt Shaker*, a students' paper which ran the usual quota of startling adolescent revelations, carefully edited by the staff representative and therefore completely innocuous. But not this time. The editor, piqued by the math teacher's flippancy, came out with a scathing article entitled "Academic Punkwood" in which he ripped apart our out-dated and largely useless course of study, and advocated topics more relevant to life. It brought down a storm of protest from above, which didn't bother the editor at all. What did bother him – and probably bothers him to this day – was that the bulk of the student body was as alarmed as was the faculty that anyone should suggest that our educational system, or indeed our entire establishment, was less than perfect.

That was in the fall of 1929. And so convinced was the teaching staff that God was on Wall Street, and all was right with the financial world, that they were into the stock-market up to their ears.

Yes, even school-teachers, traditionally the most timid members of society, were getting into the act, and if that doesn't indicate that something was wrong I don't know what would. Of course people had gone mad. They actually believed that all anyone had to do – regardless of whether they knew anything about the stock-market or not – was to buy as many stocks as possible, often on the instalment plan, and they would be rich. It was like picking money off trees. You mortgaged your house, borrowed on your insurance, sold your car, inveigled a loan from Aunt Clara, and took the plunge.

The sublime simplicity of it! Just phone your friendly broker, and tell him to buy you some stocks. Didn't much matter which. And spread the money out, please; so much down, and the balance when the stocks have doubled or tripled in value. Hurry! Hurry! Buy! Buy! Why work for money when you can get it for nothing? As often as not, the stockbroker, confident that all the stocks would go up, would take some of your money and buy stock for himself, figuring on paying you back out of his profits. It was a merry-go-round of financial bliss. Everybody could play. Even the school-teachers.

Then came that day in October when the stock-market had its worst day. The phone calls went the other way now, from broker to investor. "There's been a slight slump and we'll have to have more margin."

"But I haven't got it."

"Borrow it; sell something. You've got a big investment here, and you don't want to lose it."

"Are you sure this is just a temporary slump?"

"Of course. Listen, all the big boys are in up to their necks. They're not going to let the whole thing collapse."

"What caused it, anyway?"

"Who knows? Who cares? Just get that five hundred clams down here by tomorrow for sure!"

There was little work done in the high school classes in the following days. The physics teacher was pondering the law of physics which says "what goes up must come down". The English teacher was brooding on the quote, "We are all like swimmers in the sea . . . poised on a huge wave of fate." The history teacher couldn't get his mind off the South Sea Bubble, whose bursting in 1720 ruined thousands of Englishmen. Calamity was the name of the game.

As students, we were amused or dismayed, depending on whether or not our fathers had been hit by the crash. But like our seniors, we were confident that all would be well. Hadn't we been taught that we were the favoured of the gods? Didn't we know that ours was the best country in the world, run by the fairest government, and part of the Great British Empire, upon which the sun didn't dare to set?

We'd won the war, we knew that. We'd flogged the enemy and humiliated him beyond belief. We also knew that honesty was the best policy and spinach the best vegetable. Eat soft yeast for a clean complexion, gargle with antiseptic to ensure a breath your friends won't have to tell you about, bathe regularly in a stinking soap so there'd be no Beeohh! Go to Sunday School–and every day and in every way you'll feel better and better.

So the months went by. The sad teachers were forced to live on their salaries again, now badly slashed, and try to pay back what they'd borrowed. And somewhere, some big malevolent hand took hold of the affairs of men and squeezed the juice clear out of our lives.

We went on learning French irregular verbs, and all about the Peloponnesian War, and the binomial theorem, and the *Odes of Horace*. But we studied nothing about how to hang onto the icy top of a swaying freight car; how to lick the boots of a possible employer so that he might condescend to give us jobs at six bucks a week; how to approach a prosperous mark on the street for a handout. These things we didn't learn. Nor did we learn how to cope with malice and bigotry and hate, and the big lies that were to be the hallmark of the decade which was coming up. We didn't know, when they passed out the sealed examination papers in June of 1930, that the world was about to take a belly-flop from which it would never recover.

The good days were gone, not only the care-filled days of childhood and the mixed-up days of adolescence. Not only the naive, self-deluding time of post-war idealism, but all the old times. We were entering the grim time. The time when you'd better know which side you're on, brother. The time of the tough demagogues, and the wishful thinkers. The electronic age was about to begin, when only a handful of people in the whole world would really know what was going on. Brinksmanship was here.

Thus did we, and the world, leave behind our childhood.